Heartfelt Leadership:
Illuminating the Path to
Enlightened Success

Heartfelt Leadership
Illuminating the Path to Enlightened Success

Dr. Laura Williamson & Dr. Jivi Saran

Published by LJ Publishing
in partnership with Influence Publishing Inc., January 2024
ISBN: 978-1-7381344-0-3

Copyright © 2024 by Dr. Laura Williamson and Dr. Jivi Saran
All rights reserved. No part of this publication may be reproduced, stored in or introduced into a retrieval system, or transmitted, in any form, or by any means (electronic, mechanical, photocopying, recording or otherwise) without the prior written permission of the publisher. This book is sold subject to the condition that it shall not, by way of trade or otherwise, be lent, resold, hired out, or otherwise circulated without the publisher's prior consent in any form of binding or cover other than that in which it is published and without a similar condition including this condition being imposed on the subsequent purchaser.

Proofreading: L. Robinson
Front Cover Artwork: bestdesigns, iStock.com
Cover Design: Andrew Croft
Typesetting: Tara Eymundson

DISCLAIMERS: Readers of this publication agree that neither the authors nor their publisher will be held responsible or liable for damages that may be alleged as resulting directly or indirectly from the use of this publication. Neither the publisher nor the authors can be held accountable for the information provided by, or actions resulting from, accessing these resources.

*We dedicate this book to
every enlightened heart leader who
is working towards their state of
Eudaemonia, your maximum
potential and state of excellence.*

Table of Contents

Acknowledgments ix

Introduction xi

Maximizing Your Potential: A Guide to Utilizing the *Heartfelt Leadership* Book xvii

Chapter 1:   The Foundation of Enlightened Heart Leadership 1

Chapter 2:   Compassion and Connection 41

Chapter 3:   Mindful Communication and Interaction 55

Chapter 4:   Leading with Emotional Intelligence 63

Chapter 5:   The Power of Self-Care and Intentional Healing 67

Chapter 6:   Navigating Challenging Situations 85

Chapter 7:   Creating a Vision for the Future 107

Chapter 8:   Building Strong Teams 131

Chapter 9:   Leading Change 141

Chapter 10:   Cultivating Enlightened Heart Leadership for Positive Impact 165

Workbook: Cultivating Enlightened Heart Leadership 169

Conclusion: Using *Heartfelt Leadership* to Maximize Your Potential 179

Action Plan: Embracing Enlightened Heart Leadership 183

About the Author: Dr. Laura Williamson 187

About the Author: Dr. Jivi Saran 189

Acknowledgments

From Dr. Laura Williamson

I would like to thank my kiddos: Zoe and Maggie. I am grateful beyond measure for these two. Their intelligence, compassion, curiosity, and quick wit never cease to amaze me. They have truly taught me what it means to love. I am grateful.

I am also deeply indebted to my close friends and confidants, especially Laura, Tarsi, Orla, Katharine, Liz, and Payam. They are warriors of the spirit. I am in awe of you.

My co-author, Jivi, is a powerhouse of the heart. She and I have connected from the moment we met and forged a partnership for the ages. You, Jivi, are who and what I aspire to be. Thank you for the challenge of our friendship and collaboration. I bow to you.

I can speak for Jivi in thanking the staff of Influence Publishing. They worked with us to take our ideas and move them forward toward completion of this book. Thank you all.

Finally, I would like to thank my parents and extended family. In particular, I want to acknowledge my mother, Lisa Murphy-Perin. During the writing of this book, she passed away due to devastating injuries from a car accident on Mother's Day of this year. I hear people say that a mother will stop moving to watch her child flourish and grow. I think this might be true. She was a true believer in me. I would not be here without her and these extraordinary people. May your memory be a blessing, and thank you!

From Dr. Jivi Saran

I would like to acknowledge my children (Neena and Raj) and husband (Pete) for making this book possible, as without their support it would have been extremely challenging to achieve this amazing work. I would also like to acknowledge the loving support from my family; I believe through their kind words and compassionate check-ins, anything is possible.

I would also like to acknowledge the admiration that I have for my co-author, Laura Williamson, without whom this book was not possible. We have worked tirelessly to bring you the best of both of our worlds, and without Laura, this magical moment could not have been possible. You are seen, you are heard, and above all, my friend, you are known.

Much gratitude and love to you beyond measure.

Introduction

Enlightenment is a term used to describe a state of consciousness in which an individual has gained deep insight and understanding of the nature of reality, the self, and the world around them. It is often associated with spiritual or philosophical traditions, such as Buddhism or Hinduism, but it can also be used more broadly to describe a state of heightened awareness, understanding, and insight. Enlightenment is often characterized by a sense of inner peace, freedom from suffering, and a profound connection to the universe and all living beings. It is said to be a state of being in which one has transcended the limitations of the ego and the material world and has gained a deep understanding of the interconnectedness and oneness of all things. Achieving enlightenment is often seen as a lifelong journey that requires discipline, dedication, and practice. It is not something that can be achieved through external means or material possessions, but rather through inner work, meditation, and spiritual practice. Ultimately, enlightenment is a state of being that is characterized by wisdom, compassion, and a deep sense of interconnectedness with all things.

Enlightened heart leadership holds immense importance in today's world due to several compelling reasons. Firstly, we live in a time of complex and interconnected challenges that require holistic and inclusive solutions. Global issues such as climate change, social inequality, political polarization, and technological disruption are intertwined, demanding leaders who can navigate these complexities with wisdom and compassion. Enlightened heart leadership acknowledges the interdependence of these challenges and seeks to address them by considering the well-being of all stakeholders involved. Secondly, there is a growing emphasis on individual empowerment and the search for meaningful work and purpose. People are seeking environments where they can thrive, contribute their unique talents, and find fulfillment in their professional lives. Enlightened heart leadership responds to this by creating workplaces that prioritize employee well-being, engagement, and personal growth. It recognizes the importance of nurturing the potential of individuals and supporting their holistic development.

Furthermore, traditional models of leadership, solely based on power and authority, are being questioned in contemporary society. There is a growing demand for leaders who embody authentic values, empathy, and ethical decision-making. Enlightened heart leadership aligns with this shift by emphasizing the importance of serving others, building relationships, and inspiring positive change. It recognizes that leadership is not just about directing others but about being a role model who brings out the best in people. In addition, there is a notable shift towards conscious capitalism and a greater focus on the social and environmental impact of businesses. Enlightened heart leadership embraces this shift by emphasizing ethical business practices, social responsibility, and long-term value creation. It recognizes that businesses have a responsibility not only to generate profits but also to contribute to the well-being of society and the planet. By integrating social and environmental considerations into their decision-making, enlightened heart leaders contribute to a more sustainable and equitable future. Moreover, addressing complex challenges requires collaboration, innovation, and diverse perspectives. Enlightened heart leadership recognizes the value of collaboration and fosters inclusive and psychologically safe environments where diverse voices are heard and ideas are welcomed. It promotes a culture of learning, creativity, and adaptability, enabling organizations to navigate the rapidly changing landscape and seize opportunities for growth and innovation. Furthermore, in a world characterized by rapid change and uncertainty, building trust is essential.

Enlightened heart leadership places a strong emphasis on transparency, integrity, and open communication. By cultivating trust among team members and stakeholders, enlightened heart leaders create a foundation for strong relationships, effective collaboration, and resilience in the face of challenges. Lastly, enlightened heart leadership seeks to make a positive impact on society. It goes beyond individual and organizational success and acknowledges the interconnectedness of our world. By embodying principles such as empathy, compassion, and social responsibility, enlightened heart leaders drive positive change in their spheres of influence. They inspire others to follow suit, creating a ripple effect that can contribute to a more equitable, sustainable, and inclusive world. Enlightened heart leadership is of paramount importance in today's world. Its ability to address complex challenges, empower individuals, align with evolving expectations, embrace conscious capitalism, foster collaboration and innovation, nurture trust and resilience, and make a positive impact on society makes it a crucial leadership approach for creating a better future. By embracing the principles and practices of enlightened heart leadership, we can cultivate compassionate, sustainable, and inclusive environments that benefit individuals, organizations, and the world as a whole.

Leading with an enlightened heart refers to leading with a deep sense of awareness, compassion, and purpose. It involves using both the head and the heart to guide decision-making and interactions with others. An enlightened heart is one that is open, connected, and committed to the well-being of oneself and others. Leaders who lead with an enlightened heart prioritize empathy, compassion, and understanding in their relationships with others. They also prioritize their own self-awareness and personal growth, recognizing that their own emotional state and well-being can have a significant impact on the performance and well-being of their team. They seek to understand the perspectives and experiences of their colleagues and use this understanding to create a supportive and inclusive work environment. In addition, they are committed to a greater purpose beyond personal gain or profit. They have a clear sense of mission and vision for their organization and are dedicated to creating positive impact in the world.

Having an enlightened heart as a leader involves a range of personal qualities and behaviors that can inspire and motivate others while also fostering a positive work environment. Here are some things that leaders can do to cultivate an enlightened heart:

- Cultivate Self-Awareness: Leaders should strive to understand their own emotions, motivations, and biases. This can help them to be more empathetic and compassionate towards their team members.

- Practice Empathy: Leaders should be able to put themselves in their team members' shoes and understand their perspectives, feelings, and needs.

- Encourage Open Communication: Leaders should create an environment where team members feel comfortable expressing their ideas, concerns, and feedback.

- Lead by Example: Leaders should model the behavior they expect from their team members. They should demonstrate honesty, integrity, and respect.

- Foster a Sense of Community: Leaders should create a sense of belonging and shared purpose among their team members. This can be done by encouraging collaboration, recognizing individual contributions, and celebrating team successes.

- Continuously Learn and Grow: Leaders should seek out opportunities to learn and grow both personally and professionally. This can help them to stay current and adapt to changing circumstances.

By cultivating these qualities and behaviors, leaders can create an environment that supports the growth and development of their team members while also fostering a sense of community and shared purpose.

Having an enlightened heart as a leader is important for several reasons. Here are some of the key benefits:

- Increases Trust and Loyalty: When a leader demonstrates empathy, compassion, and understanding, it can help team members feel valued and appreciated. This, in turn, can increase trust and loyalty towards the leader and the organization.

- Improves Communication: Leaders with an enlightened heart are more likely to encourage open and honest communication among their team members. This can lead to better collaboration, problem-solving, and decision-making.

- Fosters a Positive Work Environment: When a leader creates a positive work environment, it can help team members feel motivated, engaged, and satisfied. This can lead to higher productivity and lower turnover rates.

- Enhances Creativity and Innovation: A leader who encourages creativity and innovation can help team members feel inspired and motivated to explore new ideas and approaches. This can lead to new products, services, and processes that benefit the organization.

- Enables Better Decision-Making: When a leader is open-minded, empathetic, and compassionate, they are more likely to consider diverse perspectives and make informed decisions. This can lead to better outcomes for the organization.

Defining what leadership is going forward is truly about how deeply one knows self. Going forward, leadership will see a significant shift from intellect to heart-centeredness. We've always had a male-dominated process, structure, rules, regulations, polls, profit margin, etc. We'll soon see a shift towards being open to be your entire self when you show up as a leader and not pretend to be a pseudo-self. One can be authentic, and sometimes that means that one might show some vulnerability, which traditionally, and certainly from a male leadership perspective, has never been something that is done in leadership. Historically, leadership, like patriarchy, is mind-centric, making it goal-driven. This has limitations; it will give you something and take you somewhere, but it won't help you reach your goals. To reach where you really want to go as a leader, you need to be in touch with you heart. That's why companies miss the mark constantly, and governments and people like us allow the mind to engage in heart matters, and the mind just doesn't have those skills. The mind spins us up, and as a result, we get fearful. So, the way out of fear is to give it what it needs, which is usually heart. In order to be an effective and authentic leader, it is important to understand both your heart and mind. It is critical to understand the mind and what it's doing. It's undermining you. It will do that unless you put it in its place and understand its limits, and then take time to cultivate heart and intuition to get to your how. This is like God's business versus our business.

Enlightened heart leadership is a concept that has been gaining popularity in recent years. This style of leadership emphasizes the importance of leading from a place of compassion, empathy, and mindfulness. Enlightened heart leaders are individuals who lead from a place of inner wisdom and compassion. They understand that leadership is not just about achieving success in business but also about creating positive change in the world. They prioritize the well-being of their team members, customers, and the broader community, and work to create a culture of compassion, respect, and inclusivity within their organizations. Enlightened heart leaders are also skilled in emotional intelligence, which involves the ability to recognize and manage their own emotions, as well as the emotions of others. They are able to navigate challenging situations with grace and compassion and are skilled in building strong teams that work collaboratively to achieve shared goals. Ultimately, enlightened heart leadership is about leading with a sense of purpose and meaning and working to create a better world for all. It is an approach to leadership that is rooted in mindfulness, compassion, and a deep understanding of the interconnectedness of all things. By embracing this approach to leadership, individuals can become more effective, compassionate, and purpose-driven leaders who create positive change in the world. Leaders who adopt this approach are able to create a workplace culture that fosters creativity, innovation, and overall well-being for their team members. In this book, we will explore the principles of enlightened heart leadership and how they can be applied in various contexts.

Enlightenment in leadership matters because it can help create a more compassionate, just, and sustainable world. Enlightened heart leaders can create positive change in their organizations and communities and inspire others to do the same.

Enlightened heart leaders are able to see beyond their own self-interest and work towards creating a greater good. They understand the interconnectedness of all things and the impact that their actions can have on others. This allows them to prioritize the well-being of their team members, customers, and the broader community and work towards creating a culture of compassion, respect, and inclusivity within their organizations. Enlightened heart leaders are also skilled in emotional intelligence, which enables them to navigate challenging situations with grace and compassion. They are able to manage their own emotions and those of others and create a positive and supportive work environment for their team members. This helps to build strong teams that are able to work collaboratively towards shared goals. By embracing the principles and practices of enlightened heart leadership, individuals can become more effective and compassionate leaders who create positive change in the world.

Maximizing Your Potential: A Guide to Utilizing the *Heartfelt Leadership* Book

To effectively use the *Heartfelt Leadership* book, here are some instructions to help you navigate and make the most of its contents:

- Set Your Intention: Begin by clarifying your intention for reading this book. Are you seeking personal growth, professional development, or both? Understanding your goals will guide your reading experience.

- Read Mindfully: Approach the book with an open mind and a willingness to learn. Take your time to read each chapter attentively, allowing yourself to absorb the concepts and insights presented.

- Reflect and Journal: As you progress through the book, take regular pauses to reflect on the ideas and teachings shared. Consider how they relate to your own experiences and leadership style. Maintain a journal to record your thoughts, questions, and personal reflections.

- Engage in Self-Inquiry: The book may prompt you to explore aspects of your own leadership style, values, and beliefs. Engage in self-inquiry by asking yourself questions posed in the book or formulating your own. Reflect on your answers and use them as a basis for personal growth.

- Apply the Teachings: The true value of any book lies in its application. Look for practical exercises, case studies, or actionable steps provided in the book. Actively apply the concepts in your daily life and leadership practices to experience their transformative effects.

- Seek Peer Discussions or a Study Group: If possible, join or form a study group or book club with like-minded individuals who are also reading the book. Engaging in thoughtful discussions and sharing perspectives can deepen your understanding and provide different insights.

- Experiment and Adapt: The book may offer various leadership approaches and strategies. Be open to experimenting with new ideas and adapting them to suit your unique circumstances and organizational context. Embrace the learning process and be willing to make adjustments as needed.

- Practice Self-Care: Leadership can be demanding, so remember to prioritize self-care throughout your reading journey. Take breaks when needed, engage in activities that nourish your well-being, and integrate self-reflection practices to foster a balanced approach to leadership.

- Continual Growth: Use the *Heartfelt Leadership* book as a stepping stone for ongoing personal and professional growth. Consider it a resource to revisit whenever you need inspiration, guidance, or a reminder of the principles and practices shared within.

Remember, the *Heartfelt Leadership* book is a guide, and its effectiveness ultimately lies in your willingness to engage with its teachings and apply them in your leadership journey.

CHAPTER ONE

The Foundation of Enlightened Heart Leadership

*"Avoiding danger is no safer in the long run than outright exposure.
The fearful are caught as often as the bold."*
— Helen Keller

In this chapter, we will explore the key principles that form the foundation of enlightened heart leadership. We will discuss the importance of mindfulness, empathy, compassion, and emotional intelligence in leadership. We will also explore the role of self-awareness and how it can help leaders to become more effective in their roles.

Leadership is a critical aspect of any organization, and effective leaders are essential to the success of the team. However, traditional models of leadership have been criticized for their focus on power, control, and results, often at the expense of the well-being of team members. In recent years, a new model of leadership has emerged that emphasizes compassion, empathy, and emotional intelligence. This model is known as enlightened heart leadership.

Illustration: Shutterstock

Enlightened heart leaders prioritize the well-being of their team members and recognize the importance of building strong relationships based on trust and respect. This approach is grounded in the belief that leaders can create a positive and supportive work environment that fosters innovation and creativity, leading to greater success for the organization. While the principles and practices of enlightened heart leadership can be found in many spiritual and philosophical traditions, the term itself is a modern concept. These traditions recognized that leadership was not just about achieving material success, but also about creating positive change in the world.

In the modern era, the concept of enlightened leadership has gained increasing attention, particularly in response to the growing recognition of the negative impact of traditional leadership approaches, such as the pursuit of profit at the expense of social and environmental well-being.

The term "enlightened heart leadership" was first coined by Dr. Lance Secretan, a leadership expert and author who has been at the forefront of this movement. Since then, the concept of enlightened heart leadership has gained increasing recognition and acceptance, as more and more leaders recognize the importance of leading with heart and wisdom and working towards creating positive change in the world. Today, enlightened heart leadership continues to evolve and develop, as leaders seek new ways to lead with compassion, mindfulness, and emotional intelligence.

SOUL, MIND, AND HEART

What is the signature of our soul?

Soul signature is a term used in various spiritual and metaphysical practices to describe the unique energetic imprint or essence of an individual's soul. It is the core identity that transcends the physical body and the ego. It is often said that the soul signature contains all the information and experiences that the soul has accumulated over many lifetimes. Some people may experience it as a feeling, a sense of connection, or a knowing that they are aligned with their true nature and purpose. When we are aligned with our soul signature, we are able to access our inner wisdom, intuition, and creativity. We are in a state of flow, and we feel a deep sense of fulfillment and satisfaction. We are able to connect with others on a deep level and inspire them to tap into their own inner wisdom and creativity. Enlightened heart leadership, on the other hand, is a leadership style that emphasizes empathy, compassion, and a focus on the well-being of others. It is characterized by a deep understanding of the interconnectedness of all beings and a commitment to creating positive change in the world.

An enlightened heart leader is able to connect with their soul signature and cultivate the qualities of inner wisdom, intuition, and creativity. They are able to tap into their empathy and compassion to connect with others on a deep level and inspire them to bring their best selves to their work. They are able to make decisions that are aligned with their values and the greater good, even in the face of opposition or challenge. In short, the concept of soul signature is closely related to enlightened heart leadership because it allows leaders to tap into their deepest sense of purpose and authenticity, and to lead with empathy, compassion, and a commitment to the well-being of others. Like in life, even in leadership, no one wakes up one morning and says "I wanna be a doctor" or "I wanna be an engineer; I am gonna be a leader." You become a leader by virtue of your own actions. Virtue is developed not just by intuition but by following through with your intuitions and actions. One can keep applauding until they get to negation or validation of their thoughts.

THE ROLE OF ETHICS IN ENLIGHTENED LEADERSHIP

Ethical leadership and social responsibility are pillars of enlightened leadership. By incorporating ethical principles into decision-making, fostering social responsibility, and leading with integrity, leaders can inspire trust, create positive social impact, and contribute to a sustainable future. This chapter equips leaders with the knowledge, tools, and strategies to navigate complex ethical dilemmas, champion inclusivity, and promote responsible practices. May it empower leaders to embrace ethical leadership as a fundamental aspect of their enlightened hearts, guiding their organizations towards a better world.

- Understanding Ethics in the Context of Leadership: Ethics refers to the moral principles and values that guide individuals' behavior and decision-making. In the context of leadership, ethics involves making choices that are morally right, just, and fair, considering the impact on individuals, organizations, and society as a whole. It involves aligning personal and organizational values with ethical principles to create a positive and ethical culture.

- Exploring the Link Between Ethics and the Enlightened Heart: The enlightened heart recognizes the interconnectedness of all beings and operates from a place of compassion and wisdom. Ethical leadership aligns with these qualities by demonstrating empathy, fairness, and a commitment to the well-being of all stakeholders. The enlightened heart serves as a compass for ethical decision-making and guides leaders towards actions that promote harmony, justice, and sustainable outcomes.
- The Influence of Ethical Leadership on Organizational Culture and Employee Morale: Ethical leaders set the tone for the organizational culture by modeling ethical behavior and creating a safe and trusting environment. This fosters employee morale, engagement, and loyalty. When leaders prioritize ethics, it inspires employees to act ethically and contributes to a positive work culture based on integrity and accountability.

Making Ethical Decisions

- Recognizing Ethical Dilemmas in Leadership: Ethical dilemmas arise when leaders face conflicting interests or values and there is no clear-cut solution. Leaders need to be able to identify and acknowledge these dilemmas, considering the potential consequences and ethical implications.
- Ethical Decision-Making Models and Frameworks: Various models and frameworks, such as the ethical decision-making process, can guide leaders in making ethical choices. These frameworks involve gathering relevant information, identifying alternative courses of action, evaluating their ethical implications, and selecting the option that aligns with ethical principles and values.
- Balancing Competing Interests and Values: Ethical decision-making often requires leaders to balance the needs and interests of multiple stakeholders, including employees, customers, shareholders, and the wider community. Leaders must navigate these competing interests while upholding ethical standards and

considering the long-term consequences.

- Considering Long-Term Consequences and Sustainability: Enlightened leaders adopt a long-term perspective and consider the sustainable impact of their decisions. They evaluate the potential consequences on social, environmental, and economic aspects, seeking solutions that promote the well-being of all stakeholders and future generations.

Promoting Social Responsibility and Sustainability

- Defining Social Responsibility in Leadership: Social responsibility encompasses a leader's commitment to contribute positively to society by addressing social, economic, and environmental challenges. It involves integrating social and environmental concerns into business practices and decision-making, going beyond legal obligations.

- Incorporating Sustainability Practices into Organizational Strategies: Sustainable practices aim to minimize negative impacts on the environment while fostering long-term prosperity. Leaders can integrate sustainability into strategic planning, product development, supply chain management, and resource allocation to create a positive ecological footprint.

- Engaging Stakeholders for Social and Environmental Impact: Enlightened leaders recognize the importance of engaging stakeholders, including employees, communities, customers, and NGOs, to collectively address social and environmental issues. They actively seek input, collaborate, and create partnerships to generate sustainable solutions that benefit society at large.

- Ethical Considerations in Supply Chain Management and Corporate Governance: Leaders must ensure ethical practices throughout the supply chain, including fair labor conditions, responsible sourcing, and environmental sustainability. Ethical leadership also extends to corporate governance, promoting transparency, accountability, and ethical behavior at all levels of the organization.

Leading with Integrity and Accountability

- Fostering a Culture of Integrity and Trust: Enlightened leaders prioritize creating a culture of integrity, where honesty, transparency, and ethical behavior are valued and encouraged. They lead by example, demonstrating integrity in their actions, words, and decisions.

- Setting Ethical Expectations and Standards: Leaders establish clear ethical expectations and communicate them to employees. They develop a code of ethics or conduct that outlines the organization's values, ethical standards, and expectations for behavior, serving as a guide for decision-making.

- Role Modeling Ethical Behavior as a Leader: Leaders must consistently exemplify ethical behavior in their interactions and decisions. By modeling integrity, they inspire and motivate others to adopt ethical practices, fostering a culture of trust and accountability.

- Holding Oneself and Others Accountable for Ethical Conduct: Enlightened leaders establish mechanisms to ensure accountability for ethical behavior. They implement systems for reporting unethical practices, provide channels for anonymous reporting, and take appropriate action when ethical misconduct occurs.

Addressing Ethical Challenges

- Handling Ethical Lapses and Misconduct: Ethical lapses can occur even in the most ethical environments. When ethical misconduct happens, enlightened leaders take prompt and decisive action. They investigate the situation, address the underlying causes, provide appropriate consequences, and implement measures to prevent similar occurrences in the future.

- Ethical Considerations in Navigating Conflicts of Interest: Conflicts of interest can create ethical challenges for leaders. Enlightened leaders are proactive in identifying and managing such conflicts, ensuring transparency and fairness in decision-making processes. They disclose potential conflicts, recuse themselves when necessary, and prioritize the best interests of the organization and its stakeholders.

- Encouraging Open Dialogue and Ethical Whistleblowing: Creating a culture that encourages open dialogue and ethical whistleblowing is crucial. Enlightened leaders establish channels for employees to voice ethical concerns or report misconduct without fear of retaliation. They treat whistleblowers with respect and ensure their confidentiality, fostering an environment where ethical breaches can be addressed effectively.
- Learning from Ethical Failures and Adapting Practices: When ethical failures occur, enlightened leaders view them as learning opportunities. They engage in self-reflection, identify the root causes of ethical lapses, and implement changes to prevent similar situations in the future. They promote a culture of continuous improvement and learning from mistakes.

Embracing Diversity and Inclusion

- Promoting Diversity and Inclusivity in Leadership Practices: Enlightened leaders recognize the value of diverse perspectives and actively promote diversity and inclusion within their organizations. They create inclusive environments where individuals from different backgrounds, cultures, and identities feel valued, respected, and empowered to contribute fully.
- Recognizing Biases and Unconscious Prejudices: Leaders must acknowledge and address their biases and unconscious prejudices that may influence decision-making. They foster self-awareness and engage in practices that challenge stereotypes, promote equity, and embrace diversity.
- Creating Inclusive Decision-Making Processes: Enlightened leaders involve diverse stakeholders in decision-making processes to ensure a broad range of perspectives are considered. They create platforms for open dialogue, actively seek input from underrepresented groups, and value diverse opinions.
- Leveraging Diverse Perspectives for Ethical Outcomes: Diversity fosters innovation, creativity, and ethical decision-making. Enlightened leaders leverage the diverse perspectives and experiences within their teams to identify blind spots, mitigate biases, and arrive at more comprehensive and ethical solutions.

Ethical Leadership in a Digital Age

- Ethical Considerations in the Use of Technology and Data: In the digital age, leaders must navigate ethical challenges related to data privacy, cybersecurity, and the responsible use of emerging technologies. They establish guidelines for ethical data collection, usage, and protection, ensuring compliance with regulations and respecting individuals' privacy rights.

- Ensuring Privacy and Data Protection: Enlightened leaders prioritize protecting individuals' privacy and ensuring data security. They establish robust data protection measures, transparent data handling practices, and clear consent mechanisms to maintain trust with customers, employees, and other stakeholders.

- Addressing Digital Ethics and Cyber Threats: Leaders must be vigilant about potential ethical dilemmas arising from the use of technology. They proactively address issues such as algorithmic biases, the responsible use of artificial intelligence, and the ethical implications of automation. They establish protocols to mitigate cyber threats and protect sensitive information.

- Building Trust in the Digital Realm through Ethical Leadership: In a world increasingly reliant on digital platforms, enlightened leaders cultivate trust by championing ethical leadership practices in the digital realm. They prioritize transparency, integrity, and accountability in their organizations' digital initiatives, fostering trust among stakeholders.

Engaging in Corporate Citizenship

- Encouraging Community Engagement and Volunteerism: Enlightened leaders recognize the importance of giving back to the communities in which they operate. They encourage employees to engage in community service and volunteer activities, aligning corporate resources with community needs.

- Partnering with Nonprofit Organizations for Social Impact: Collaboration with nonprofit organizations allows leaders to leverage their expertise and resources for social impact. Enlightened leaders seek strategic partnerships with nonprofits that align with their organization's mission and values, working together to address social and environmental challenges.

- Leveraging Corporate Resources for Philanthropic Initiatives: Leaders have the opportunity to make a difference through philanthropic initiatives. They allocate resources, including financial contributions, in ways that address pressing social issues and support education, healthcare, environmental conservation and other causes aligned with their organizational values.
- Aligning Organizational Values with Corporate Social Responsibility: Enlightened leaders ensure that corporate social responsibility (CSR) efforts are not mere gestures but a reflection of the organization's values and commitment to societal well-being. They align CSR initiatives with the organization's purpose, engaging employees and stakeholders in meaningful ways.

Ethical Leadership in Times of Crisis

- Navigating Ethical Challenges During Crises: Crises often present leaders with unique ethical challenges. Enlightened leaders demonstrate composure, empathy, and ethical decision-making in times of uncertainty. They prioritize the well-being and safety of stakeholders while upholding ethical principles.
- Balancing Organizational Priorities and Stakeholder Welfare: During a crisis, leaders face the challenge of balancing the needs of the organization with the welfare of stakeholders. Enlightened leaders navigate this delicate balance by making decisions that prioritize the long-term sustainability and ethical well-being of all involved parties.
- Communicating Ethically and Transparently in Difficult Situations: Open and transparent communication is essential during crises. Enlightened leaders provide accurate information, address concerns promptly, and communicate with empathy and integrity. They establish channels for dialogue, listen to stakeholders' perspectives, and make ethical decisions based on the best available information.
- Rebuilding Trust and Reputation through Ethical Leadership: In the aftermath of

a crisis, rebuilding trust and reputation is paramount. Enlightened leaders take responsibility for any shortcomings, learn from the experience, and implement measures to prevent similar crises in the future. They demonstrate unwavering commitment to ethical leadership, rebuilding trust through consistent ethical behavior and transparent communication.

Sustaining Ethical Leadership Practices

- Creating Ethical Systems and Structures within Organizations: Enlightened leaders establish structures and systems that support ethical behavior. This includes implementing ethical policies, establishing compliance mechanisms, providing ethics training, and fostering a culture that values ethics and accountability.

- Providing Ethical Leadership Development and Training: Leaders must continuously develop their ethical leadership skills. Enlightened leaders invest in ongoing training and development programs that cultivate ethical decision-making, moral reasoning, and emotional intelligence. They encourage leaders at all levels to engage in self-reflection and personal growth to enhance their ethical leadership capabilities.

- Celebrating Ethical Achievements and Promoting Best Practices: Recognizing and celebrating ethical achievements reinforces the importance of ethical behavior. Enlightened leaders acknowledge and reward individuals and teams that exemplify ethical leadership. They share best practices, stories, and case studies that inspire others to follow ethical principles.

- Embedding Ethical Considerations into Strategic Planning and Decision-Making: Enlightened leaders ensure that ethics is an integral part of strategic planning and decision-making processes. They incorporate ethical considerations into goal-setting, risk assessments, and resource allocation, aligning organizational strategies with ethical values and long-term sustainability.

There are multifaceted aspects of ethical leadership and social responsibility that offer insights, frameworks, and practical strategies for leaders to achieve an enlightened heart. By embracing ethics, leaders can create a culture of integrity, promote social responsibility, and navigate complex challenges with wisdom and compassion. May this knowledge empower leaders to lead with an enlightened heart, fostering positive change and making a lasting impact on individuals, organizations, and society as a whole.

The new success factors—spiritual intelligence, emotional intelligence, self-governance, and sovereignty—would lead to the type of leadership we describe. We need to build a self-governing, self-sustaining nation within ourselves to be able to lead other people. Self-identity is the soul signature. Spiritual intelligence is a level of self-sovereignty and emotional intelligence. Self-governance of the mind is vital to draw the boundaries to keep negative, harmful thoughts away and only keep thoughts that help you grow. People support themselves not just financially but also emotionally, spiritually, and physically. It's like a double-edged sword. We don't want to be a self-centered egocentric, but the more those facets are addressed, the less they need.

Becoming an enlightened leader is not a destination but a lifelong journey. By cultivating an enlightened heart, leaders can unlock their full potential and positively impact the lives of those they lead. This book serves as a guide, offering insights, practical strategies, and inspiring stories to support leaders in their quest for enlightened leadership. May it inspire and empower leaders to embrace their innate wisdom, compassion, and authenticity, fostering a brighter and more enlightened future for all.

THE MIND IS THE DRIVER

In the pursuit of enlightened leadership, cultivating mindfulness holds significant value. Mindfulness is the practice of being fully present, aware, and nonjudgmental in the current moment. This essay explores the essential role of mindfulness in nurturing an enlightened heart and its profound impact on leadership effectiveness. By integrating mindfulness into their leadership approach, leaders can enhance self-awareness, empathy, decision-making, and overall well-being. Mindfulness serves as a powerful tool for leaders seeking to cultivate an enlightened heart. By embracing mindfulness practices, leaders can deepen self-awareness, nurture empathy, enhance decision-making, and foster well-being within themselves and their organizations. Mindful leaders embody the qualities of presence, compassion, and wisdom, inspiring others to thrive and creating a positive impact in the world. May this chapter encourage leaders to integrate mindfulness into their leadership journey, nurturing an enlightened heart and transforming their organizations into beacons of mindful and compassionate leadership. When you start practicing mindfulness, you will start to witness a shift that occurs within yourself. Practicing thought control teaches the validity of thoughts. We systemize mental constructs within seconds; we look at something and build a mental construct almost instantly.

Understanding Mindfulness in Leadership

- Defining Mindfulness and Its Relevance to Leadership: Mindfulness is the practice of intentionally paying attention to the present moment without judgment. In leadership, mindfulness involves being fully present in interactions, making conscious choices, and cultivating a deep understanding of oneself and others.
- Exploring the Connection between Mindfulness and the Enlightened Heart: Mindfulness is an essential component of the enlightened heart as it allows leaders to connect with their inner wisdom, compassion, and authenticity. By cultivating mindfulness, leaders can access their innate qualities of empathy, wisdom, and ethical decision-making.
- The Benefits of Incorporating Mindfulness into Leadership Practices: Mindfulness enhances leadership effectiveness by improving self-awareness, emotional intelligence, decision-making, and communication skills. It also reduces stress, increases resilience, and promotes well-being for both leaders and their teams.

Cultivating Self-Awareness through Mindfulness

- Developing an Inner Awareness of Thoughts, Emotions, and Behaviors: Mindfulness practices such as meditation, breath awareness, and body scanning help leaders observe their thoughts, emotions, and patterns of behavior without judgment. This self-awareness enables leaders to understand their strengths, weaknesses, and triggers, leading to greater self-mastery.
- Recognizing Personal Biases and Habitual Patterns: Mindfulness allows leaders to recognize their biases, prejudices, and automatic responses. By bringing awareness to these patterns, leaders can transcend them and make more conscious and

unbiased decisions.
- Embracing Self-Reflection as a Tool for Growth and Self-Improvement: Mindfulness encourages leaders to engage in regular self-reflection and introspection. This practice fosters continuous learning, personal growth, and the development of leadership competencies.
- Harnessing Mindfulness to Enhance Emotional Intelligence: Mindfulness cultivates emotional intelligence by developing the ability to recognize and regulate emotions, empathize with others, and respond to situations with wisdom and compassion.

Empathy and Compassion in Enlightened Leadership

- Cultivating Empathy through Mindfulness Practices: Mindfulness deepens leaders' capacity for empathy by helping them tune in to others' experiences and perspectives. Through mindful listening and observing, leaders can develop a genuine understanding of their team members' needs, concerns, and aspirations.
- Developing a Deep Understanding of Others' Perspectives and Emotions: Mindfulness allows leaders to suspend judgment and truly listen to others' viewpoints. By cultivating empathy and compassion, leaders create a safe and inclusive environment where everyone's voice is heard and respected.
- Demonstrating Compassion and Empathy in Leadership Interactions: Mindful leaders exhibit compassion by responding to others' emotions with kindness, understanding, and support. They create a culture of care and foster meaningful connections that promote collaboration, trust, and well-being.
- Nurturing a Culture of Empathy and Care within the Organization: Mindful leaders establish practices and initiatives that prioritize empathy and care within the organizational culture. This may include empathy training, team-building exercises, and fostering a supportive work environment that values and encourages empathy and compassion.

Enhancing Decision-Making through Mindfulness

- Utilizing Mindfulness to Improve Clarity and Focus: Mindfulness practices enhance leaders' ability to focus their attention and concentrate on the task at hand. This focused awareness allows leaders to make decisions based on a clear understanding of the situation and the broader impact of their choices.

- Making Conscious and Informed Decisions: Mindfulness helps leaders make decisions with greater intentionality and awareness. By observing their thoughts, emotions, and biases, leaders can discern the most ethical, sustainable, and compassionate course of action.

- Balancing Analytical Thinking with Intuitive Wisdom: Mindfulness allows leaders to integrate rational analysis with intuitive insights. By accessing their inner wisdom, leaders can tap into a deeper level of understanding and make decisions that align with their values and the greater good.

- Leveraging Mindfulness to Manage Uncertainty and Complexity: Mindfulness equips leaders with the resilience and adaptability needed to navigate uncertainty and complexity. By staying present, leaders can respond effectively to changing circumstances, remain flexible in their decision-making, and inspire confidence in their teams.

Mindfulness for Effective Communication and Collaboration

- Listening with Presence and Deep Attention: Mindful leaders actively listen to others with their full presence and undivided attention. They set aside distractions, suspend judgment, and create a safe space for open and honest communication.

- Practicing Mindful Communication to Foster Understanding and Connection: Mindful leaders communicate with intention, clarity, and empathy. They choose their words carefully, consider the impact of their communication, and adjust their approach to ensure messages are understood and received positively.

- Resolving conflicts with Compassion and Nonjudgment: Mindfulness enables leaders to approach conflicts with compassion, seeking understanding rather than assigning blame. They cultivate a nonjudgmental mindset, promote dialogue, and facilitate collaborative problem-solving to resolve conflicts and build stronger relationships.

- Using Mindfulness to Build Strong Relationships and Collaborative Teams: Mindfulness enhances leaders' ability to build trust, empathy, and rapport with team members. By recognizing and valuing diverse perspectives, mindful leaders create an inclusive environment where everyone feels respected, heard, and motivated to contribute their best.

Stress Reduction and Well-Being in Leadership

- Managing Stress and Burnout through Mindfulness Practices: Mindfulness helps leaders manage stress by cultivating resilience, reducing reactivity, and promoting self-care. Regular mindfulness practices, such as meditation, breathing exercises, and mindful movement, enable leaders to recharge and maintain their well-being.

- Developing Resilience and Adaptability in the Face of Challenges: Mindfulness equips leaders with the mental and emotional resilience needed to navigate challenges effectively. By staying present, leaders can respond to setbacks with equanimity, learn from adversity, and inspire their teams to persevere.

- Nurturing Self-Care and Work-Life Balance: Mindful leaders prioritize self-care and encourage work-life balance within their teams. They model healthy boundaries, promote self-care practices, and create a culture that values employee well-being as a foundation for sustainable high performance.

- Creating a Culture of Well-Being within the Organization: Mindful leaders foster a culture that prioritizes well-being by implementing wellness programs, offering resources for stress reduction and self-care, and promoting a healthy work environment. They recognize that employee well-being is essential for organizational success and cultivate a supportive culture that values the whole person.

Mindful Leadership in Challenging Times

- Applying Mindfulness During Times of Crisis and Uncertainty: Mindfulness empowers leaders to stay grounded and composed during challenging times. By cultivating mindfulness, leaders can manage their own fears and anxieties, make thoughtful decisions, and provide stability and reassurance to their teams.

- Cultivating Equanimity and Maintaining a Steady Presence: Mindful leaders develop equanimity, the ability to remain calm and composed amidst turbulence. They anchor themselves in the present moment, respond rather than react, and inspire confidence in others through their unwavering presence.

- Making Ethical Decisions with Clarity and Wisdom: Mindfulness enables leaders to make ethical decisions with heightened clarity and wisdom. By connecting with their values and ethical principles, leaders can navigate complex situations, consider the impact of their choices, and act in alignment with their enlightened heart.

- Inspiring and Guiding Others through Mindful Leadership Practices: Mindful leaders inspire and guide others by modeling mindfulness and leading with authenticity, empathy, and compassion. They offer support, encourage self-care, and provide a sense of direction and purpose during challenging times.

Integrating Mindfulness into Organizational Culture

- Creating a Mindful Organizational Culture through Leadership Examples: Mindful leaders set an example by embodying mindfulness in their own actions, decisions, and interactions. Their behavior influences the broader organizational culture and encourages others to embrace mindfulness as well.

- Incorporating Mindfulness Practices into Daily Routines and Rituals: Mindful leaders integrate mindfulness practices into the daily routines and rituals of the organization. This may include starting meetings with a brief mindfulness exercise, establishing designated quiet spaces for reflection, or incorporating mindfulness breaks into the workday.

- Offering Mindfulness Training and Resources for Employees: Mindful leaders provide opportunities for employees to learn and develop mindfulness skills. They offer mindfulness training programs, workshops, and resources to support employees' personal growth, well-being, and professional development.

- Sustaining Mindfulness Practices through Ongoing Support and Reinforcement: Mindful leaders foster a culture of sustainability by providing ongoing support and reinforcement for mindfulness practices. This may involve establishing mindfulness communities, assigning mindfulness mentors, or incorporating mindfulness into performance evaluations and recognition programs.

Mindfulness as a Catalyst for Organizational Transformation

- Harnessing Mindfulness to Drive Organizational Change Initiatives: Mindfulness can be a catalyst for organizational transformation by promoting openness, adaptability, and innovative thinking. Mindful leaders use mindfulness practices to create a culture of continuous improvement and inspire change initiatives that align with the organization's purpose and values.

- Fostering Innovation and Creativity through a Mindful Approach: Mindfulness enhances leaders' capacity to think creatively, embrace ambiguity, and encourage diverse perspectives. By cultivating a mindful approach to problem-solving and decision-making, leaders create an environment that fosters innovation, curiosity, and learning.

- Creating a Values-Driven and Purpose-Oriented Organization: Mindful leaders connect their teams to a shared sense of purpose and align their actions with the organization's values. By integrating mindfulness into the fabric of the organization, leaders ensure that decisions, strategies, and initiatives are driven by ethical principles and contribute to the greater good.

- Inspiring a Shared Sense of Purpose and Meaning among Employees: Mindful leaders inspire employees by connecting them to a sense of purpose and meaning in their work. They create opportunities for employees to explore their values, align their work with their personal aspirations, and foster a sense of fulfillment and engagement.

Personal Growth and Continual Development

- Cultivating a Lifelong Commitment to Mindfulness and Personal Growth: Mindful leaders recognize that mindfulness is a lifelong journey and commit to their ongoing personal growth. They engage in regular mindfulness practices, seek further training and development opportunities, and continuously evolve as leaders.

- Embracing a Beginner's Mind and Openness to Learning: Mindful leaders adopt a beginner's mind, approaching each experience with curiosity, openness, and a willingness to learn. They cultivate a growth mindset, embrace feedback, and remain receptive to new ideas and perspectives.

- Seeking Opportunities for Self-Development and Self-Mastery: Mindful leaders actively seek opportunities for self-development and self-mastery. They engage in leadership development programs, seek mentors or coaches, and invest in their own well-being and personal growth.

- Evolving as an Enlightened Leader through Ongoing Mindfulness Practice: Mindful leaders understand that their journey toward enlightened leadership is a continuous process. By maintaining a consistent mindfulness practice, leaders deepen their connection with their enlightened heart, cultivate their leadership presence, and evolve as compassionate, wise, and impactful leaders.

Mindfulness serves as a transformative force in enlightened leadership. By integrating mindfulness practices into their leadership approach, leaders can enhance self-awareness, empathy, decision-making, and overall well-being. Mindfulness is a state of awareness that involves being present and attentive to the current moment. It is a key component of enlightened heart leadership because it helps leaders to stay focused and present in their interactions with team members. By practicing mindfulness, leaders can better understand their own thoughts and emotions, which can help them to make better decisions and respond more effectively to challenges and conflicts. Empathy is the ability to understand and share the feelings of another person. In leadership, empathy is critical because it helps leaders to build stronger relationships with their team members. When leaders demonstrate empathy, team members feel heard and understood, which can lead to greater trust and cooperation. By putting themselves in the shoes of their team members, leaders can make more informed decisions that consider the needs and perspectives of everyone involved. Compassion is the desire to alleviate the suffering of others. In leadership, compassion involves treating team members with kindness, respect, and understanding. When leaders demonstrate compassion, they create a positive and supportive work environment that fosters greater job satisfaction and higher levels of engagement. This, in turn, can lead to better productivity and greater success for the organization. Emotional intelligence is the ability to understand and manage one's own emotions, as well as the emotions of others. It is a critical component of enlightened heart leadership because it helps leaders to better understand themselves and their team members. By developing emotional intelligence, leaders can make better decisions, communicate more effectively, and build stronger relationships. Self-awareness is the ability to understand one's own thoughts, feelings, and behaviors. It is a critical component of enlightened heart leadership because it helps leaders to recognize their own strengths and weaknesses. By being aware of their own limitations, leaders can better delegate tasks, seek input from others, and make better decisions. Mindful leaders create a culture that values presence, compassion, and wisdom, inspiring positive change and nurturing the growth and development of their teams. May this chapter inspire leaders to embrace mindfulness as a foundation for cultivating an enlightened heart and creating a lasting impact on individuals, organizations, and society as a whole.

THE HEART

In enlightened heart leadership, the heart plays a pivotal role as the center of wisdom, compassion, and authenticity. It represents the seat of emotional intelligence and the source of ethical decision-making. The heart is not merely a physical organ but symbolizes the core essence of a leader's being and the wellspring of their connection with others.

- Authenticity and Emotional Intelligence: The heart in enlightened leadership encompasses authenticity and emotional intelligence. Leaders with an enlightened heart lead from a place of genuine authenticity, embracing their true selves and allowing their actions to be guided by their core values and principles. By connecting with their own emotions and understanding the emotions of others, they cultivate emotional intelligence, which enables them to empathize, inspire, and create meaningful connections with their team members.

- Compassion and Empathy: The heart in enlightened leadership embodies compassion and empathy. Leaders with an enlightened heart possess a deep sense of care, concern, and empathy for others. They genuinely understand and resonate with the experiences, challenges, and aspirations of their team members. Through their compassionate nature, they create a safe and inclusive environment where everyone feels valued, supported, and empowered to reach their full potential.

- Wisdom and Ethical Decision-Making: The heart in enlightened leadership represents wisdom and ethical decision-making. Leaders with an enlightened heart tap into their inner wisdom, intuition, and moral compass to make decisions that are aligned with their values and principles. They go beyond purely rational analysis and consider the broader impact of their choices on individuals, organizations, and society. The heart serves as a guide, reminding leaders to act with integrity, fairness, and a deep sense of responsibility.

- Connection and Collaboration: The heart in enlightened leadership fosters connection and collaboration. Leaders with an enlightened heart recognize the interconnectedness of all beings and the importance of building relationships based on trust, respect, and collaboration. They nurture a sense of unity and foster a collective purpose, bringing people together to work towards shared goals. Through their enlightened heart leadership, they create an environment where collaboration flourishes, and individuals feel a sense of belonging and collective ownership.

- Inspiration and Transformation: The heart in enlightened leadership inspires and catalyzes transformation. Leaders with an enlightened heart lead by example, radiating their passion, purpose, and positive energy. Their authentic presence and genuine care inspire and motivate others to strive for excellence, personal growth, and positive change. By embodying the qualities of an enlightened heart, leaders become agents of transformation, influencing individuals, organizations, and even society at large.

The heart in enlightened heart leadership represents the seat of wisdom, compassion, authenticity, and ethical decision-making. It is the source of emotional intelligence, empathy, connection, inspiration, and transformation. Leaders who cultivate an enlightened heart lead with integrity, empathy, and a deep sense of purpose, creating a positive impact on individuals, organizations, and the world. The heart is truly a witness, and the muscle is the detachment from your thoughts, both as mental and heart construct. Both the heart and mind have their own place. A leader's job is to truly understand if it is the mind or the heart at play. Mind is a useful and powerful tool; one can engage their heart through meditation and mindfulness.

Understanding what the binding agent is for your mind and heart is essential. Through this, we aim to get to leadership's underlying essence. Our minds are capable of having over 60,000 of the same thoughts every day. However, just because you have a thought doesn't make it true. In general, people fail to understand the nature of how the mind works. The mind regurgitates the same thoughts, and it's our job to discern. Leaders need to have a bigger, broader way of being to pull people into an experience where they also show up more fully aware of themselves. That's really the trick. One can't give something one doesn't have. The seat of wisdom in enlightened heart leadership refers to the deep well of inner wisdom, insight, and intuition that leaders tap into when making decisions and navigating complex situations. It is a place within oneself where knowledge, experience, and a sense of interconnectedness converge to guide leaders towards wise and ethical choices.

- Intuitive Knowing: The seat of wisdom is associated with intuitive knowing, which goes beyond rational analysis and logical thinking. Leaders with an enlightened heart cultivate the ability to listen to their inner voice, trusting their instincts and gut feelings when faced with difficult decisions. This intuitive knowing is often based on a deep understanding of oneself, others, and the broader context in which decisions are made.

- Holistic Perspective: The seat of wisdom enables leaders to take a holistic perspective, considering multiple dimensions of a situation. They go beyond the immediate circumstances and delve into the underlying causes and long-term consequences of their actions. By accessing their inner wisdom, leaders can see the interconnectedness of various factors and make decisions that align with the greater good, taking into account the well-being of individuals, teams, organizations, and society as a whole.

- Transcending Ego: The seat of wisdom involves transcending ego-driven motivations and personal biases. Leaders with an enlightened heart recognize that ego-based desires and attachments can cloud judgment and hinder ethical decision-making. By accessing the seat of wisdom, leaders can detach themselves from their own self-interests and ego-driven desires, enabling them to make decisions that are guided by higher principles and values.

- Ethical Reflection: The seat of wisdom encourages leaders to engage in deep ethical reflection. Leaders reflect upon their values, principles, and the potential impact of their decisions on stakeholders. They consider questions such as: "What is the right thing to do?" "How will this decision affect others?" and "Does this decision align with my values and the values of the organization?" This reflective process helps leaders make ethical choices that are aligned with their enlightened heart.

- Continuous Learning: The seat of wisdom is also associated with a mindset of continuous learning and growth. Leaders with an enlightened heart recognize that wisdom is not a fixed state but an ongoing journey of exploration and development. They remain open to new perspectives, seek feedback and diverse viewpoints, and engage in lifelong learning to expand their understanding and deepen their wisdom.

- Integration of Head and Heart: The seat of wisdom involves the integration of rational thinking and emotional intelligence. It is not solely about relying on intellectual analysis or emotional responses but about balancing the insights of both the head and the heart. Leaders with an enlightened heart leverage their analytical thinking skills while staying connected to their emotions and the needs of others, creating a harmonious integration that guides their decision-making process.

- Connection with Universal Truths: The seat of wisdom connects leaders to universal truths and timeless principles. It transcends cultural and individual biases, enabling leaders to tap into a deeper understanding of what is just, fair, and morally right. Leaders access universal truths through introspection, reflection, and contemplative practices, aligning their actions with these guiding principles. In enlightened heart leadership, the seat of wisdom represents a deep reservoir of insight, intuition, and ethical understanding. By accessing this seat, leaders make wise and compassionate decisions that benefit not only themselves but also their teams, organizations, and the wider world. It is through the integration of wisdom with compassion that enlightened heart leaders create a positive impact and inspire others to reach their fullest potential. It's a collective of everything that happens within us that formulates the standard operating procedure of how you operate in the world.

LEADERSHIP IN ACTION

In the journey towards enlightened heart leadership, learning plays a vital role. Learning is not merely acquiring knowledge or skills; it is a transformative process that expands our understanding, deepens our self-awareness, and nurtures the qualities of an enlightened heart.

This essay explores the profound relationship between learning and enlightened heart leadership, highlighting how learning fuels personal growth, cultivates wisdom, and inspires compassionate action. Learning is also a result of a socialization factor. We are guided intentionally or unintentionally by the social construct built around us. We learn from interacting with each other, our partners, and everybody in the world. Everything also constantly gives us messages on how we should think and feel, and there's an impact there as well. As a leader, you have team members whose standard operating procedures clash with each other or the follower as well as the leader, given the situation. It's a tripod: the leader, the follower, and the situation. So if the situation is not occurring, the leadership skills will not be tested. Personal values and ethics are only tested when the rubber hits the road. However, it is important to note that values and ethics are situational too.

The Power of Curiosity and Openness to Learning

- Embracing a Growth Mindset: Enlightened heart leaders embody a growth mindset, recognizing that their potential for growth and development is limitless. They approach learning with curiosity and a thirst for knowledge, continuously seeking new insights and perspectives to broaden their understanding.

- Embracing the Unknown: Enlightened heart leaders embrace the unknown and step outside their comfort zones. They recognize that true learning happens when they venture into unfamiliar territory, challenging their assumptions and exploring new possibilities.
- Cultivating Humility: Learning requires humility, as it involves acknowledging that there is always more to discover and that others may hold valuable wisdom. Enlightened heart leaders cultivate humility, recognizing that they are lifelong learners who can benefit from the diverse experiences and perspectives of others.

Self-Reflection and Inner Growth

- Cultivating Self-Awareness: Learning in the context of enlightened heart leadership begins with self-reflection and self-awareness. Leaders embark on a journey of introspection, examining their values, beliefs, and biases. They develop an understanding of their strengths, limitations, and areas for growth, fostering a deeper connection with their authentic selves.
- Emotional Intelligence: Learning encompasses the development of emotional intelligence, which involves understanding and managing one's emotions and empathizing with others. Enlightened heart leaders learn to navigate their own emotions, cultivating self-regulation and empathy to create a supportive and compassionate leadership environment.
- Unraveling Limiting Beliefs: Learning involves questioning and unraveling limiting beliefs that may hinder personal and leadership growth. Enlightened heart leaders challenge their own assumptions and embrace new perspectives, allowing for transformative shifts in thinking and behavior.

Wisdom as the Fruit of Learning

- Integrating Knowledge and Experience: Learning involves integrating knowledge gained through study and experience. Enlightened heart leaders synthesize their learnings, merging theoretical concepts with practical wisdom to inform their decision-making and leadership approach.

- Cultivating Discernment and Critical Thinking: Learning nurtures discernment and critical-thinking skills, enabling leaders to evaluate information, recognize biases, and make well-informed decisions. Enlightened heart leaders approach learning with a discerning mind, cultivating the ability to extract essential insights from diverse sources.
- Integrating Head and Heart: Enlightened heart leaders integrate intellectual knowledge with the wisdom of the heart. They balance rational thinking with emotional intelligence, using their intellectual understanding as a foundation for compassionate action and ethical decision-making.

Learning as a Catalyst for Compassionate Action

- Cultivating Empathy and Compassion: Learning fosters empathy and compassion, enabling leaders to connect deeply with the experiences and needs of others. Enlightened heart leaders learn to view situations from multiple perspectives, expanding their capacity for empathy and inspiring compassionate action.
- Social and Environmental Consciousness: Learning expands leaders' awareness of social and environmental challenges, inspiring them to become agents of positive change. Enlightened heart leaders seek to understand systemic issues, engage in socially responsible practices, and take actions that contribute to the well-being of communities and the environment.
- Lifelong Learning as a Source of Inspiration: Enlightened heart leaders embrace lifelong learning as a source of inspiration and motivation. They continuously seek opportunities for personal and professional growth, engaging in further education, mentorship, and self-reflection to continually deepen their wisdom and expand their impact.

Creating a Learning Culture

- Fostering a Culture of Learning: Enlightened heart leaders create a culture that values learning, growth, and personal development. They foster an environment where curiosity is encouraged, mistakes are seen as opportunities for growth, and continuous learning is embedded in the organization's DNA.

- Providing Learning Opportunities: Enlightened heart leaders provide diverse learning opportunities for their teams. They invest in training programs, workshops, conferences, and coaching to support their employees' development, nurturing a collective commitment to growth and learning.
- Encouraging Reflection and Knowledge Sharing: Enlightened heart leaders encourage reflection and knowledge sharing within their teams. They create spaces for dialogue, encourage open communication, and facilitate opportunities for individuals to share their learnings and insights with others.

Learning and enlightened heart leadership are deeply intertwined. Learning fuels personal growth, cultivates wisdom, and inspires compassionate action. By embracing a growth mindset, self-reflection, and a commitment to ongoing learning, leaders can foster an enlightened heart that guides their decisions, relationships, and contributions to the world. May this chapter inspire leaders to embrace learning as a transformative journey and cultivate an enlightened heart that positively impacts themselves, their teams, and the greater community.

WHAT IS LEADERSHIP GOING FORWARD?

The world is evolving at an unprecedented pace, demanding a new paradigm of leadership that goes beyond traditional models. As we look to the future, enlightened heart leadership emerges as a powerful approach that can navigate the complexities of the modern world with wisdom, compassion, and authenticity. This essay explores the future of leadership through the lens of enlightened heart, highlighting the transformative potential it holds for individuals, organizations, and society.

Embracing Complexity and Uncertainty

- Adaptive Mindset: The future of leadership requires an adaptive mindset that embraces complexity and uncertainty. Enlightened heart leaders have the capacity to navigate ambiguity, recognize emerging patterns, and make informed decisions in rapidly changing environments. They lead with flexibility, resilience, and the ability to inspire others to adapt and thrive in dynamic contexts.

- Systems Thinking: Enlightened heart leaders adopt a systems-thinking approach, recognizing the interconnectedness and interdependencies of various elements within organizations and the broader world. They understand that decisions and actions have ripple effects, and they strive to create positive outcomes for all stakeholders. By considering the holistic picture, enlightened heart leaders can address complex challenges and foster sustainable growth.

Purpose-Driven Leadership

- Authentic Purpose: Enlightened heart leaders recognize the importance of leading with a clear and authentic purpose. They align their personal values with the purpose of the organization, guiding their actions and inspiring others with a shared sense of meaning and direction. Purpose-driven leadership fosters a sense of fulfillment and resilience, enabling leaders to navigate challenges with unwavering dedication.
- Ethical Leadership: The future of leadership demands a strong ethical foundation. Enlightened heart leaders prioritize ethics and integrity in their decision-making processes. They consider the long-term impact of their choices on individuals, communities, and the planet, placing a high value on fairness, justice, and social responsibility. By leading ethically, they cultivate trust, foster sustainable relationships, and build organizations that are guided by moral principles.

Collaboration and Inclusivity

- Collective Intelligence: Enlightened heart leaders understand the power of collective intelligence and collaboration. They create an inclusive and diverse environment where ideas are openly shared and individuals feel valued and empowered to contribute their unique perspectives. They foster a culture of collaboration, leveraging the collective wisdom of their teams to solve complex problems and drive innovation.

- Stakeholder Engagement: Enlightened heart leaders go beyond focusing solely on shareholders and embrace a broader view of stakeholders. They engage with employees, customers, communities, and other relevant parties to understand their needs, aspirations, and concerns. By considering diverse perspectives and incorporating stakeholder voices, enlightened heart leaders make decisions that are sustainable and beneficial for all.

Emotional Intelligence and Empathy

- Emotional Resilience: The future of leadership requires emotional intelligence and resilience. Enlightened heart leaders possess self-awareness, self-regulation, and empathy, allowing them to navigate and manage their emotions effectively. They also extend empathy to others, fostering a compassionate and supportive work environment where individuals feel understood and valued.
- Empowering Others: Enlightened heart leaders empower their teams by fostering a culture of psychological safety and growth. They create opportunities for individuals to develop their skills, talents, and potential. By investing in the growth and well-being of their employees, enlightened heart leaders cultivate a motivated and engaged workforce that drives organizational success.

Lifelong Learning and Adaptability

- Continuous Learning: Enlightened heart leaders recognize that learning is a lifelong journey. They embrace a mindset of continuous learning, seeking new knowledge, insights, and skills to stay relevant in an ever-evolving world. They encourage their teams to engage in ongoing learning and provide resources and support for personal and professional development.
- Adaptive Leadership: Enlightened heart leaders are adaptable and agile. They embrace change as an opportunity for growth and transformation. They encourage experimentation, innovation, and the willingness to take calculated risks. Through their adaptive leadership style, they inspire others to embrace change, learn from setbacks, and proactively adapt to emerging trends and challenges.

The future of leadership lies in the embrace of enlightened heart principles. By cultivating wisdom, compassion, authenticity, and adaptability, leaders can navigate the complexities of the modern world and inspire positive change. The enlightened heart approach not only brings about personal and organizational success but also has the potential to contribute to the greater well-being of individuals, communities, and the planet. As we step into the future, may enlightened heart leaders pave the way for a more inclusive, sustainable, and harmonious world.

THE INNER JOURNEY OF SELF-EXCELLENCE

Enlightened heart leadership is not only about leading others; it starts with leading oneself. In this section, we explore the concept of self-excellence within the context of enlightened heart leadership. Self-excellence refers to the ongoing pursuit of personal growth, self-mastery, and the cultivation of one's inner qualities. By embodying self-excellence, leaders can develop the inner foundation necessary to lead with wisdom, compassion, and authenticity.

- Self-Awareness: Self-excellence begins with self-awareness. Enlightened heart leaders undertake an inner journey to understand their values, strengths, weaknesses, triggers, and aspirations. They cultivate deep self-reflection, mindfulness, and introspection to gain clarity about their authentic selves.
- Personal Growth: Self-excellence is a lifelong commitment to personal growth and development. Enlightened heart leaders continuously seek opportunities to expand their knowledge, skills, and perspectives. They engage in self-study, attend workshops, seek mentorship, and embrace challenges that stretch their capabilities.

Cultivating Inner Qualities

- Emotional Intelligence: Enlightened heart leaders cultivate emotional intelligence—the ability to understand, manage, and empathize with their own emotions and the emotions of others. They develop emotional self-awareness, self-regulation, empathy, and effective relationship management, fostering healthy and authentic connections with their teams.
- Resilience: Self-excellence requires resilience—the capacity to bounce back from

setbacks, face challenges, and maintain a positive mindset in the face of adversity. Enlightened heart leaders cultivate resilience through self-care, mindfulness practices, seeking support when needed, and developing a growth-oriented mindset.

- Integrity and Authenticity: Enlightened heart leaders prioritize integrity and authenticity in their actions and interactions. They align their behaviors with their values and lead with transparency, honesty, and consistency. By embodying authenticity, they inspire trust and create a safe and supportive environment for others to be their true selves.

Balancing Self-Care and Service

- Self-Care: Enlightened heart leaders recognize the importance of self-care. They understand that taking care of their physical, mental, and emotional well-being is vital for sustainable leadership. They prioritize self-care practices such as exercise, adequate rest, mindfulness, healthy relationships, and pursuing hobbies and passions.
- Service-Oriented Leadership: While self-excellence focuses on personal growth, enlightened heart leaders understand that leadership is ultimately about service to others. They cultivate a deep sense of purpose and dedication to making a positive impact on individuals, communities, and the world. They lead with empathy, compassion, and a genuine desire to uplift and empower others.

Continuous Reflection and Learning

- Reflective Practices: Enlightened heart leaders engage in regular reflection to evaluate their actions, decisions, and impact. They journal, meditate, and create dedicated time for self-reflection. Through reflection, they gain insights, identify areas for growth, and make course corrections to align with their enlightened heart principles.
- Lifelong Learning: Self-excellence is inseparable from lifelong learning. Enlightened heart leaders embrace a growth mindset and actively seek opportunities to

expand their knowledge and skills. They read books, attend seminars, participate in conferences, and engage in conversations with diverse individuals to broaden their perspectives. People should realize that they can move towards the pursuit of self-excellence. We must recognize that mortality is natural and acknowledge the invisible expiry date on our bodies. That hidden expiry date on our bodies dictates our choices and decisions. We come fully equipped to be that magnificent and brilliant person we were born as, as long as we are willing to do the work and move into conscious awareness. When people are aligned, their brilliance shows up, and they won't have to work at it. One must realize and understand their authentic self. This leads to one being able to make their own decisions and have the strength to follow their truth. By building up self-esteem to have the confidence to recognize their choices versus others' choices, one aligns with their excellence. The gut never guides you wrong. If one is in tune with their gut, it will never steer them wrong. It'll always tell you what is in alignment with who you are. Like our external listening ears, we also need to keep our internal listening ears on to listen to our gut. We should give it the attention and recognition that it deserves. We can't even hear it with all the other noise sometimes. So, it is essential to ground and center ourselves within the noise and chaos around us to pursue self-excellence.

Self-excellence is a foundational element of enlightened heart leadership. By embarking on the inner journey of self-awareness, cultivating inner qualities, balancing self-care and service, and embracing continuous reflection and learning, leaders can develop the inner reservoirs necessary for enlightened heart leadership. By cultivating self-excellence, leaders not only become more effective in their roles but also inspire and uplift others, creating a positive and transformative impact on individuals, organizations, and society as a whole. May this section inspire leaders to embark on the path of self-excellence, recognizing its profound significance in enlightened heart leadership.

WHAT ARE THE BOUNDARY LINES OF SELF-IDENTITY?

Self-identity, the understanding of oneself, plays a fundamental role in shaping our thoughts, actions, and interactions. In the context of leadership, self-identity deeply influences the way leaders perceive themselves, relate to others, and make decisions. This section explores the intricate relationship between self-identity and enlightened heart leadership, delving into how a strong and aligned sense of self contributes to compassionate, authentic, and impactful leadership.

The Formation of Self-Identity

- Nature and Nurture: Self-identity is shaped by a combination of genetic predispositions and environmental factors. It emerges through a complex interplay between one's innate characteristics and the influences of family, culture, education, and life experiences.

- Core Beliefs and Values: Core beliefs and values form the foundation of self-identity. These deeply held convictions define our principles, guide our behaviors, and shape our perceptions of the world. Enlightened heart leaders reflect on their core beliefs and values, ensuring they are aligned with principles of compassion, integrity, and a genuine desire to serve others.

Self-Identity and Authentic Leadership

- Authenticity: Authentic leadership stems from a strong and congruent self-identity. Enlightened heart leaders embrace their true selves and lead with transparency, genuineness, and vulnerability. They are comfortable with their strengths and imperfections, allowing them to connect with others on a deep and meaningful level.

- Emotional Intelligence: Self-identity influences emotional intelligence—the ability to recognize, understand, and manage one's own emotions and the emotions of others. Enlightened heart leaders develop emotional self-awareness, which enables them to respond empathetically, regulate their emotions, and foster healthy relationships with their teams.

The Role of Self-Identity in Compassionate Leadership

- Empathy and Compassion: Self-identity influences one's capacity for empathy and compassion. Enlightened heart leaders develop a compassionate self-identity by cultivating empathy, actively listening to others, and seeking to understand diverse perspectives. They lead with kindness, empathy, and a genuine concern for the well-being of others.

- Servant Leadership: A strong self-identity is foundational to servant leadership—a leadership philosophy centered on selflessness and service to others. Enlightened heart leaders with a clear self-identity understand their purpose and commit themselves to uplifting and empowering others. They prioritize the growth and well-being of their team members above personal gain.

Overcoming Identity Challenges

- Ego and Identity Attachment: The ego often influences self-identity, leading to attachment and identification with external factors such as status, power, or material possessions. Enlightened heart leaders recognize the pitfalls of ego-driven identity and actively work towards transcending egoic tendencies. They detach their self-worth from external validation, focusing instead on inner qualities and the impact they create.

- Embracing Diversity and Inclusion: Self-identity can influence how leaders perceive and engage with diversity. Enlightened heart leaders develop a broad and inclusive self-identity that embraces diversity in all its forms. They foster an inclusive environment where diverse perspectives are valued, contributing to creativity, innovation, and holistic decision-making.

Self-Identity and Ethical Decision-Making

- Moral Integrity: Self-identity plays a crucial role in ethical decision-making. Enlightened heart leaders with a well-defined self-identity anchored in moral integrity are more likely to make principled and ethical choices. They align their actions with their core values and prioritize the greater good, even in challenging circumstances.

- Ethical Responsibility: Leaders with a strong self-identity recognize their ethical responsibility towards stakeholders, communities, and the environment. They consider the impact of their decisions on various stakeholders and strive to act in a manner that is fair, just, and socially responsible.

Nurturing and Evolving Self-Identity

- Self-Reflection: Enlightened heart leaders engage in regular self-reflection to deepen their understanding of self-identity. They set aside dedicated time for introspection, journaling, and contemplation, allowing them to explore their values, motivations, and aspirations.
- Lifelong Learning: Self-identity evolves through continuous learning and growth. Enlightened heart leaders embrace lifelong learning, seeking new experiences, acquiring new knowledge, and engaging in personal and professional development opportunities. They remain open-minded and adaptable, embracing change as a catalyst for personal transformation.

Self-identity is a powerful force that shapes enlightened heart leadership. Leaders who understand and cultivate a strong, authentic, and compassionate self-identity are better equipped to navigate challenges, inspire others, and create positive change. By embracing self-reflection, nurturing moral integrity, and embracing diversity, leaders can develop a self-identity that serves as a guiding light in their leadership journey. May this chapter inspire leaders to embark on a profound exploration of self-identity, unlocking their potential to lead with wisdom, compassion, and authenticity. Enlightened heart leadership is closely related to self-identity because it involves a deep understanding and acceptance of one's own values, beliefs, and purpose. When we are able to connect with our true self and cultivate a sense of inner wisdom and intuition, we are better able to lead with empathy and compassion and make decisions that are aligned with our values. Enlightened heart leadership requires a certain level of self-awareness and self-reflection. It involves taking the time to reflect on our own beliefs, biases, and assumptions and to become aware of the impact that these may have on our leadership style and decision-making. This process of self-reflection and self-awareness allows us to identify and work through any blocks or limitations that may be preventing us from fully embodying our true self.

Self-identity is closely related to our values and beliefs, and these are central to the concept of enlightened heart leadership. When we are able to connect with our true self and understand our values and purpose, we are better able to lead with authenticity and inspire others to do the same. Our self-identity shapes our leadership style and decision-making, and it is an essential aspect of effective and heart-centered leadership. In essence, enlightened heart leadership is about leading from a place of inner wisdom and authenticity, and this requires a deep understanding and acceptance of our own self-identity. By connecting with our true self and cultivating a sense of inner wisdom and intuition, we are able to lead with empathy, compassion, and a commitment to the well-being of others, while staying true to our own values and purpose. There's still a collective; we are still part of a collective. So you have to know the boundary lines of: "Although I'm an individual, I'm a part of a collective, and as a part of a community, who am I?" Know the limits of the mind; it's a useful tool, but it is just a tool. Learn to cultivate energies to quiet the mind and to keep it in its place, you can pull it out like a calculator. It's good at math, so put it back when you're done calculating.

WHAT ARE THE STEPS ONE MUST TAKE TO GET THERE?

Enlightened heart leadership is a leadership approach that is rooted in empathy, compassion, and a focus on the well-being of others. It is a leadership style that emphasizes the interconnectedness of all beings and a commitment to creating positive change in the world. At its core, enlightened heart leadership is about leading from a place of inner wisdom and authenticity. To achieve enlightened heart leadership, there are several key aspects that leaders must focus on. First and foremost, it requires a deep understanding and acceptance of one's own values, beliefs, and purpose. Leaders must take the time to reflect on their own biases, assumptions, and limitations and become aware of the impact that these may have on their leadership style and decision-making. In addition to self-reflection and self-awareness, enlightened heart leadership also requires a commitment to empathy and compassion. Leaders must cultivate the ability to connect with others on a deep level, to listen to their needs and concerns, and to respond with kindness and understanding. This requires a willingness to put aside ego and self-interest and to focus on the well-being of others.

Another important aspect of enlightened heart leadership is the ability to make decisions that are aligned with one's values and the greater good. This means having the courage to stand up for what is right, even in the face of opposition or challenge. It means being willing to take risks, to challenge the status quo, and to embrace innovation and creativity.

To achieve enlightened heart leadership, leaders must also cultivate a sense of inner wisdom and intuition. This involves developing a deep connection with one's soul signature and tapping into the inner guidance and creativity that comes from this connection. It means trusting one's intuition and being willing to take inspired action, even if it is not immediately clear how it will lead to the desired outcome. Finally, enlightened heart leadership requires a commitment to continuous learning and growth. This means seeking out new knowledge, skills, and perspectives, and being willing to challenge one's own assumptions and biases. It means embracing feedback and constructive criticism and using this as an opportunity to learn and improve. Enlightened heart leadership is a leadership approach that emphasizes empathy, compassion, and a focus on the well-being of others. To achieve it, leaders must cultivate a deep understanding and acceptance of their own values and purpose, as well as a commitment to empathy and compassion, aligned decision-making, inner wisdom and intuition, and continuous learning and growth. By embodying these key aspects, leaders can create positive change in the world and inspire others to do the same.

Step 1: Self-Reflection and Awareness

- Engage in regular self-reflection practices, such as journaling, meditation, or contemplation, to deepen self-awareness and understand personal values, beliefs, strengths, and areas for growth.
- Seek feedback from trusted mentors, peers, or coaches to gain insights into blind spots and areas for improvement.
- Explore personal triggers, biases, and assumptions that may hinder compassionate and authentic leadership.

Step 2: Cultivating Inner Qualities

- Develop emotional intelligence by enhancing self-awareness, self-regulation, empathy, and effective relationship management.
- Cultivate resilience by practicing self-care, embracing challenges, and maintaining a positive mindset in the face of adversity.
- Foster integrity and authenticity by aligning actions with values, leading transparently, and embracing vulnerability.

Step 3: Continuous Learning and Growth

- Embrace a growth mindset and commit to lifelong learning. Seek out books, seminars, workshops, or online courses to expand knowledge, skills, and perspectives.
- Engage in ongoing professional and personal development opportunities to enhance leadership competencies and gain new insights.
- Actively seek feedback and be open to constructive criticism as a means for growth and improvement.

Step 4: Empathy and Compassion

- Cultivate empathy by actively listening, seeking to understand others' perspectives, and practicing empathy in daily interactions.
- Foster a compassionate mindset by showing kindness, empathy, and genuine concern for the well-being of others.
- Encourage a culture of empathy and compassion within the team or organization by modeling these behaviors and promoting understanding and support.

Step 5: Ethical Decision-Making

- Develop a strong moral compass by clarifying personal values and ethical principles.
- Prioritize ethical considerations in decision-making processes, considering the

impact on all stakeholders and the broader society.
- Seek guidance or ethical frameworks when facing complex or challenging decisions to ensure alignment with enlightened heart principles.

Step 6: Collaboration and Inclusivity

- Foster a collaborative and inclusive work environment where diverse perspectives are valued and respected.
- Actively seek input from team members and stakeholders to promote participatory decision-making and co-creation.
- Create opportunities for collaboration, teamwork, and knowledge sharing to harness collective intelligence and promote innovation.

Step 7: Service-Oriented Leadership

- Embrace a servant-leadership mindset focused on serving others, uplifting and empowering team members, and fostering their growth and development.
- Prioritize the well-being and success of others over personal gain or recognition.
- Lead with humility and a genuine desire to make a positive impact on individuals, communities, and the world.

Step 8: Continuous Reflection and Adaptation

- Regularly evaluate and reflect on personal leadership practices, seeking areas for improvement and growth.
- Embrace feedback as a valuable source of learning and adjust leadership approaches accordingly.
- Remain adaptable and open to change, embracing emerging trends and adjusting leadership strategies to meet evolving challenges.

Step 9: Seek Support and Mentorship

- Seek guidance and support from mentors, coaches, or like-minded leaders who embody enlightened heart leadership principles.
- Engage in peer learning groups or communities to share experiences, challenges, and best practices.
- Actively seek opportunities for mentorship and mentor others to foster a culture of continuous growth and development.

Step 10: Lead by Example

- Model enlightened heart leadership principles in daily actions, interactions, and decision-making.
- Inspire and motivate others through your own commitment to personal growth, authenticity, empathy, and ethical leadership.
- Continuously reinforce the values and principles of enlightened heart leadership through communication, recognition, and creating a supportive organizational culture.

Remember, achieving enlightened heart leadership is an ongoing journey that requires commitment, self-reflection, and continuous growth. By following this action plan and consistently applying these principles, you can cultivate a leadership style that embodies wisdom, compassion, authenticity, and positive impact.

In the following chapters, we will explore the practical applications of these principles in various leadership contexts, providing readers with a comprehensive understanding of how to become more effective and compassionate leaders.

CHAPTER TWO

Compassion and Connection

"You don't get harmony when everybody sings the same note."
— Doug Floyd

Enlightened heart leadership goes beyond the individual leaders; it extends to the very fabric of the corporate culture within an organization. In today's dynamic and interconnected world, organizations are recognizing the importance of fostering an enlightened heart culture that values compassion, integrity, and social responsibility. This chapter explores the key elements that contribute to such a culture, highlighting the significance of shared values, purpose-driven orientation, authentic leadership, empowerment, collaboration, well-being, continuous learning, and social and environmental responsibility. By understanding and cultivating these elements, organizations can create an environment that nurtures the growth and well-being of their employees, while also making a positive impact on society and the world.

Illustration: Shutterstock

Shared Values and Purpose

- Clearly Defined Values: An enlightened heart corporate culture is anchored in clearly defined values that guide decision-making, behavior, and interactions. These values reflect compassion, integrity, respect, and social responsibility.
- Purpose-Driven Orientation: Organizations with an enlightened heart culture align their activities and goals with a broader purpose beyond financial success. They foster a sense of shared purpose, emphasizing how their work contributes to the well-being of individuals, society, and the planet.

Authentic Leadership

- Transparent and Genuine Leadership: Enlightened heart corporate cultures are led by authentic leaders who demonstrate transparency, vulnerability, and a commitment to ethical behavior. They foster trust and build meaningful connections with employees.
- Leading by Example: Leaders in an enlightened heart culture model the values and principles they expect from their employees. They prioritize empathy, compassion, and a service-oriented mindset, inspiring others to do the same.

Empowerment and Collaboration

- Employee Empowerment: An enlightened heart culture empowers employees by fostering an environment of trust, autonomy, and accountability. Employees are encouraged to contribute their ideas, take ownership of their work, and make meaningful decisions.
- Collaborative Decision-Making: Organizations with an enlightened heart culture prioritize collaborative decision-making, involving employees at all levels. They recognize the diverse perspectives and collective intelligence that arise from inclusive decision-making processes.

Well-Being and Work-Life Balance

- Holistic Well-Being: Enlightened heart cultures prioritize the well-being of their employees by offering programs and initiatives that support physical, mental, and emotional health. This includes providing wellness resources, flexible work arrangements, and promoting work-life balance.

- Supportive Environment: Organizations foster a supportive environment that recognizes the personal and professional needs of employees. They promote open communication, provide resources for personal development, and encourage a healthy work-life integration.

Continuous Learning and Growth

- Learning Culture: Enlightened heart corporate cultures embrace a culture of continuous learning, providing opportunities for professional development, skill enhancement, and knowledge sharing. They encourage a growth mindset and support employees in their pursuit of personal and professional growth.

- Innovation and Adaptability: Organizations with an enlightened heart culture foster an environment that encourages innovation, creativity, and adaptability. They promote a willingness to take calculated risks, learn from failures, and adapt to changing circumstances.

Social and Environmental Responsibility

- Social Impact: Enlightened heart cultures emphasize social responsibility and contribute positively to the communities they serve. They engage in philanthropy, volunteerism, and social initiatives aligned with their values and purpose.

- Environmental Stewardship: Organizations with an enlightened heart culture prioritize environmental sustainability. They implement eco-friendly practices, reduce their carbon footprint, and support initiatives that promote environmental conservation.

An enlightened heart corporate culture encompasses shared values, purpose-driven orientation, authentic leadership, empowerment, collaboration, well-being, continuous learning, and social and environmental responsibility. By cultivating these key elements, organizations can create a positive, inclusive, and purposeful environment that supports the growth and well-being of their employees while making a meaningful impact on society and the planet. May this chapter inspire organizations to embrace enlightened heart principles and build corporate cultures that embody compassion, authenticity, and sustainable success.

THE IMPORTANCE OF COMPASSION IN THE WORKPLACE

Compassion is the ability to understand and empathize with the feelings of others and to respond with kindness and support. In this chapter, we will explore the importance of creating a culture of compassion in the workplace and how leaders can promote compassion among their team members. Compassion is an essential quality in any workplace. When people feel that they are valued and supported by their colleagues and superiors, they are more likely to be engaged, motivated, and committed to their work. Compassion creates a positive work environment that fosters trust, respect, and collaboration. In this essay, we will explore the importance of compassion in the workplace and how it can be cultivated.

Firstly, compassion creates a sense of connection and belonging. When people feel that they are part of a community, they are more likely to feel invested in the success of the organization and the well-being of their colleagues. A workplace culture that values compassion encourages team members to build positive relationships with each other, share their experiences, and support each other through challenges. Secondly, compassion improves well-being and reduces stress. When employees feel that they are supported by their colleagues and superiors, they are less likely to experience stress and burnout. Compassionate workplaces prioritize the mental and emotional well-being of their employees and provide resources and support to help them manage stress and maintain a healthy work-life balance. Thirdly, compassion improves productivity and performance. When people feel valued and supported, they are more likely to be engaged and motivated in their work. Compassionate leaders are able to inspire their team members to give their best effort and work collaboratively towards shared goals. Compassionate workplaces also prioritize ongoing learning and development, providing opportunities for employees to enhance their skills and knowledge. Finally, compassion is critical in creating a positive reputation for an organization. When people perceive an organization as compassionate and supportive, they are more likely to be attracted to it as a place to work or do business. Compassionate organizations are also more likely to attract and retain top talent, as people are drawn to workplaces that prioritize well-being, collaboration, and positive impact.

To cultivate compassion in the workplace, organizations can implement several strategies. Firstly, they can prioritize the well-being of their employees by offering benefits and resources that support mental and emotional health. Secondly, they can prioritize ongoing learning and development, providing opportunities for employees to enhance their skills and knowledge. Thirdly, they can encourage team members to build positive relationships with each other by fostering a culture of collaboration, respect, and empathy. Finally, they can lead by example, modeling compassionate behavior and creating a positive work environment for their team members. Compassion is an essential quality in any workplace. It creates a sense of connection and belonging, improves well-being and reduces stress, enhances productivity and performance, and creates a positive reputation for an organization. To cultivate compassion in the workplace, organizations can prioritize employee well-being, ongoing learning and development, positive relationships, and leading by example.

Creating a Culture of Compassion

Enlightened heart leadership and compassion are intimately connected. Compassion is the foundation of enlightened heart leadership, and it is a critical element in creating a positive and impactful leadership style. Compassion is defined as the ability to connect with others on a deep level, to feel their pain and suffering, and to respond with kindness and understanding. Compassionate leaders are able to put aside their own ego and self-interest and focus on the well-being of others. They are able to create a safe and supportive environment where individuals feel valued, respected, and heard.

In enlightened heart leadership, compassion is not just a nice-to-have quality. It is an essential element of effective leadership. When leaders are able to connect with their team members on a deep level, they are better able to understand their needs and concerns and to respond in a way that is supportive and empowering. This creates a sense of trust and respect and helps to build a strong and cohesive team. Compassionate leaders are also able to create a culture of empathy and understanding. They are able to model the behavior they want to see in others and create an environment where individuals feel comfortable sharing their own experiences and perspectives. This allows for greater creativity and innovation and helps to foster a sense of belonging and connection. In addition to its impact on team dynamics, compassion is also critical in creating positive change in the world. Compassionate leaders are able to see beyond their own needs and desires and focus on the needs of others. They are able to create a vision for a better world and inspire others to join them in making this vision a reality. Enlightened heart leadership and compassion also go hand in hand in terms of personal growth and development. When leaders are able to cultivate compassion, they are better able to connect with their own inner wisdom and intuition. They are able to recognize their own biases and limitations and work through these to become more effective and heart-centered leaders.

Enlightened heart leadership and compassion are closely connected. Compassion is an essential element of effective leadership, and it is critical in creating a supportive and empowering team environment. Compassionate leaders are able to create positive change in the world and inspire others to join them in this journey. By cultivating compassion, leaders can connect with their own inner wisdom and intuition and become more effective and heart-centered leaders.

Creating a culture of compassion starts with the leader. Leaders must model compassionate behavior and make it clear that compassion is a core value of the organization. This can be done by showing empathy for team members, listening actively, and responding with kindness and support. Leaders can also promote a culture of compassion by encouraging team members to support one another. This can be done by creating opportunities for team members to connect with one another, such as team-building activities or social events. Leaders can also encourage team members to offer support to one another during difficult times, such as when a team member is dealing with a personal issue. In addition, leaders can promote a culture of compassion by providing resources and support for team members. This can include offering mental health resources, such as counseling or therapy, as well as flexible work arrangements for team members who may be dealing with personal or family issues.

Enlightened heart leaders prioritize compassion and empathy in their leadership style. They understand that creating a culture of compassion in the workplace is essential for building a positive and supportive environment that fosters trust, respect, and collaboration. In this essay, we will explore how enlightened heart leaders create a culture of compassion.

Firstly, enlightened heart leaders model compassionate behavior. They lead by example, demonstrating empathy and kindness towards their team members and creating a positive work environment that encourages compassion and understanding. They are mindful of their own actions and behaviors and are intentional in their interactions with others. Secondly, enlightened heart leaders prioritize communication. They are open and transparent with their team members and encourage open and honest communication throughout the organization. They actively listen to the perspectives and concerns of their team members and respond with empathy and understanding. Thirdly, enlightened heart leaders prioritize the well-being of their team members. They understand that when employees feel valued and supported, they are more likely to be engaged and productive in their work. They prioritize mental and emotional health and provide resources and support to help their team members manage stress and maintain a healthy work-life balance. Fourthly, enlightened heart leaders create a culture of collaboration. They encourage their team members to work together towards shared goals and value the diverse perspectives and experiences of their team members. They foster a sense of community and belonging and provide opportunities for team members to build positive relationships with each other. Finally, enlightened heart leaders prioritize ongoing learning and development. They understand that in order to create a culture of compassion, it is important for team members to continuously enhance their skills and knowledge. They provide opportunities for training and development and encourage team members to learn from each other and share their experiences. Enlightened heart leaders create a culture of compassion by modeling compassionate behavior, prioritizing communication, prioritizing the well-being of their team members, creating a culture of collaboration, and prioritizing ongoing learning and development. By doing so, they create a positive and supportive work environment that fosters trust, respect, and collaboration, and enables team members to thrive both personally and professionally.

Overcoming Barriers to Compassion

Enlightened heart leaders prioritize compassion and empathy in their leadership style. However, there may be barriers that can hinder their ability to cultivate a culture of compassion in the workplace. In this essay, we will explore some of the barriers to compassion enlightened heart leaders experience, and how they can overcome them. Firstly, one of the barriers to compassion is a lack of time and resources. In today's fast-paced work environment, leaders may feel pressure to prioritize productivity and efficiency over compassion and empathy. However, enlightened heart leaders understand the importance of creating a culture of compassion, and they make it a priority to dedicate time and resources to support their team members' well-being and foster positive relationships. They may delegate tasks, prioritize goals, or reorganize their schedules to make time for compassionate leadership. Secondly, another barrier to compassion is a lack of understanding or awareness. Sometimes leaders may not understand the impact of their behavior on their team members or may not be aware of the challenges their team members are facing. To overcome this barrier, enlightened heart leaders prioritize open and honest communication with their team members, actively listen to their concerns, and seek feedback regularly. They may also invest in training and education to enhance their understanding of compassion and empathy and how to apply them in the workplace. Thirdly, another barrier to compassion is a lack of trust or respect between team members. When there is conflict or tension among team members, it can be difficult for leaders to create a culture of compassion. To overcome this barrier, enlightened heart leaders prioritize building trust and respect among team members. They may facilitate team-building activities, encourage open communication, and promote a culture of inclusivity and diversity. Fourthly, another barrier to compassion is a lack of self-awareness. Sometimes leaders may be unaware of their own biases or negative behavior patterns that hinder their ability to be compassionate and empathetic. To overcome this barrier, enlightened heart leaders prioritize self-reflection and personal growth. They may seek feedback from their team members or colleagues, practice mindfulness or meditation, or invest in personal development programs.

In conclusion, enlightened heart leaders may face barriers to cultivating a culture of compassion in the workplace. However, by prioritizing time and resources, seeking to understand and be aware of their team members' needs, building trust and respect among team members, and prioritizing self-awareness and personal growth, they can overcome these barriers and create a positive and supportive work environment that fosters compassion, empathy, and collaboration.

Creating a culture of compassion is not always easy. There may be barriers, such as a lack of trust or a competitive work environment, that can make it difficult to promote compassion among team members. However, with persistence and commitment, these barriers can be overcome.

Leaders can overcome barriers to compassion by building trust with their team members. This can be done by being transparent, honest, and consistent in their actions and communications. Leaders can also work to reduce competition among team members by emphasizing collaboration and teamwork. Compassion is a core value of enlightened heart leadership, and creating a culture of compassion is essential for promoting a positive and supportive work environment. By modeling compassionate behavior, encouraging team members to support one another, and providing resources and support, leaders can create a workplace culture that fosters empathy, kindness, and understanding.

SUSTAINMENT

Sustainment is a central concept that is closely related to the idea of Dharma, which refers to fulfilling one's duty and responsibilities in a way that promotes the well-being of oneself, others, and the environment. Sustainment is considered a fundamental principle, as it emphasizes the need to maintain balance and harmony in all aspects of life. Enlightened heart leadership, which prioritizes compassion, empathy, and sustainability, is consistent with the principles of sustainment. Dharma, derived from ancient Indian philosophies and spiritual traditions, holds a profound significance in enlightened heart leadership. Dharma refers to an individual's inherent nature, purpose, and duty, encompassing principles of righteousness, ethical conduct, and the pursuit of one's true calling. In this article, we delve into the role of Dharma in enlightened heart leadership, exploring how it guides leaders to align their actions with higher values, make ethical decisions, embrace authenticity, and foster a service-oriented mindset. By understanding and embodying Dharma, leaders can cultivate a transformative leadership approach that not only benefits their organizations but also creates a positive impact on individuals, communities, and the world.

Alignment with Higher Values

- Dharma as a Moral Compass: Dharma serves as a moral compass for enlightened heart leaders, guiding their actions, decisions, and behaviors. It encourages leaders to align with values such as compassion, integrity, fairness, and social responsibility, ensuring that their leadership is grounded in ethical principles.

- Interconnectedness and Oneness: Dharma reminds leaders of the interconnectedness of all beings and the interdependence of the world. It encourages leaders to view their role in a broader context, making decisions that consider the well-being of all stakeholders and contribute to the greater good.

Ethical Decision-Making

- Dharma-Based Ethics: Dharma provides a framework for ethical decision-making. It calls upon leaders to prioritize moral integrity, honesty, transparency, and fairness in their choices, even in complex or challenging situations. Dharma-driven leaders consider the consequences of their actions and strive to minimize harm while promoting justice and well-being.
- Balancing Personal and Organizational Values: Dharma helps leaders navigate the delicate balance between personal values and the values of the organization. Enlightened heart leaders ensure that their personal Dharma aligns with the organization's mission and values, creating harmony between their individual purpose and the collective purpose of the organization.

Authenticity and Personal Fulfillment

- Understanding Personal Dharma: Dharma encourages leaders to explore and understand their unique purpose, talents, and passions. By embracing their personal Dharma, leaders gain clarity about their authentic selves and align their leadership approach with their inner values, leading to a deep sense of fulfillment and personal satisfaction.
- Inspiring Others through Authenticity: Dharma-driven leaders inspire others by authentically living their values and purpose. By embracing their true calling and demonstrating authenticity, leaders inspire trust, motivate their teams, and create a culture where individuals feel empowered to embrace their own unique path.

Service-Oriented Leadership

- The Essence of Service: Dharma instills a service-oriented mindset in enlightened heart leaders. They view leadership as a means to serve others, focusing on the well-being, growth, and success of their team members, stakeholders, and the broader society. Service-oriented leaders prioritize the needs of others over personal gain or recognition.

- Empowering and Uplifting Others: Dharma-driven leaders empower their team members, providing them with the necessary support, resources, and opportunities for growth. They create a nurturing environment that fosters collaboration, personal development, and the realization of individual potential.

Personal Growth and Self-Reflection

- Dharma as a Catalyst for Personal Growth: Dharma encourages leaders to engage in self-reflection, introspection, and continuous personal growth. It prompts leaders to regularly assess their actions, motivations, and impact, seeking opportunities for improvement, learning, and self-transformation.

- Mindfulness and Consciousness: Dharma emphasizes the importance of mindfulness and cultivating a deep awareness of one's thoughts, emotions, and actions. Enlightened heart leaders practice mindfulness, enabling them to make conscious choices, respond with wisdom and compassion, and build meaningful connections with others.

Dharma plays a pivotal role in enlightened heart leadership, guiding leaders to align their actions with higher values, make ethical decisions, embrace authenticity, and foster a service-oriented mindset. By embodying Dharma, leaders create a transformative leadership approach that benefits their organizations, empowers their teams, and contributes to the well-being of individuals, communities, and the world. As leaders embrace their personal Dharma and embody the principles of enlightened heart leadership, they become catalysts for positive change, inspiring others to live their values and pursue their higher purpose. May this chapter inspire leaders to embrace Dharma as a guiding principle, fostering a new paradigm of leadership that embodies compassion, integrity, and profound impact.

The following are some ways in which enlightened heart leadership relates to sustainment:

- Balance and Harmony: Enlightened heart leaders prioritize balance and harmony in their decision-making processes, recognizing that all aspects of life are interconnected. This is consistent with the concept of Dharma, which emphasizes the need to maintain balance and harmony between the individual, the society, and the environment.
- Service to Others: Enlightened heart leaders prioritize service to others, recognizing that their actions have a ripple effect on the well-being of others. This is consistent with the concept of *seva*, which refers to selfless service to others and the community.
- Environmental Sustainability: Enlightened heart leaders prioritize environmental sustainability, recognizing that their actions have an impact on the environment and future generations. This is consistent with the concept of *prakriti*, which refers to the natural world and the need to protect and preserve it for future generations.
- Ethical Behavior: Enlightened heart leaders prioritize ethical behavior, recognizing that their actions have consequences for themselves and others. This is consistent with the concept of karma, which emphasizes the need to act in accordance with one's Dharma and to accept the consequences of one's actions.

Enlightened heart leadership is consistent with the principles of sustainment from the perspective of Hinduism. It emphasizes the need to maintain balance and harmony, prioritize service to others, promote environmental sustainability, and act with ethical behavior. By prioritizing these principles, enlightened heart leaders can create a positive and sustainable work environment that benefits all stakeholders and the environment. People, ultimately, do desire love, affection, and connection. However, having that demand come from an external force isn't viable, yet that is what we seek. In reality, the external environment is just an impression of the internal environment. It is essential to connect yourself with your internal environment. The problem is that people either get disconnected from themselves or were never connected to begin with. This is because humans operate using only 5 percent of their consciousness. Part of the solution to this problem is operating from a connected place, which is with an enlightened heart. This reveals also that our community provides us with social and cognitive learning, where we learn from one another, not just from ourselves. We need to understand how we connect with the community and how we can help each other move forward to make sure we experience the connection of sharing. All of this works together to create an environment rich for diversity and inclusion.

CHAPTER THREE

Mindful Communication and Interaction

*"It strikes! one, two, Three, four, five, six. Enough, enough, dear watch,
Thy pulse hath beat enough. Now sleep and rest; Would thou could'st make
the time to do so too; I'll wind thee up no more."*
— Ben Jonson

Enlightened heart leadership is closely related to mindfulness, as both concepts emphasize the importance of being present, aware, and compassionate in one's actions and decision-making.

Mindfulness refers to the practice of being present and aware of one's thoughts, feelings, and surroundings in a nonjudgmental way. It emphasizes the importance of paying attention to the present moment and being fully engaged in one's actions and interactions with others.

Enlightened heart leadership, on the other hand, emphasizes the importance of compassion, empathy, and sustainability in leadership. It recognizes that leadership is not just about achieving financial goals but also about creating a positive impact on employees, stakeholders, and the environment.

Illustration: Shutterstock

The following are some ways in which enlightened heart leadership relates to mindfulness:

- Presence and Awareness: Enlightened heart leaders practice presence and awareness in their decision-making, recognizing the importance of being fully engaged in the present moment. This is consistent with the mindfulness practice of being present and aware of one's thoughts and feelings in a nonjudgmental way.
- Compassionate Leadership: Enlightened heart leaders prioritize compassion and empathy in their interactions with others, recognizing the importance of understanding and acknowledging the emotions and experiences of others. This is consistent with the mindfulness practice of being compassionate and nonjudgmental towards oneself and others.
- Sustainable Decision-Making: Enlightened heart leaders prioritize sustainability in their decision-making, recognizing the importance of considering the long-term impact of their actions on the environment, stakeholders, and future generations. This is consistent with the mindfulness practice of being aware of the interconnectedness of all things and the importance of considering the impact of one's actions on others.
- Mindful Communication: Enlightened heart leaders practice mindful communication, recognizing the importance of clear and effective communication in promoting understanding, trust, and collaboration. This is consistent with the mindfulness practice of being aware of one's words and how they impact others.

Mindful communication and enlightened heart leadership are closely related as both concepts emphasize the importance of clear, effective, and compassionate communication in building trust, promoting understanding, and creating a positive work environment. The following are some ways in which mindful communication is related to enlightened heart leadership:

- Compassionate Communication: Enlightened heart leaders prioritize compassionate communication, recognizing the importance of being empathetic, understanding, and nonjudgmental in their interactions with others. This involves active listening, acknowledging the emotions and experiences of others, and responding with empathy and compassion. Mindful communication similarly emphasizes the importance of nonjudgmental listening and speaking with empathy and compassion.

- Effective Communication: Enlightened heart leaders prioritize effective communication, recognizing the importance of clear and concise communication in promoting understanding and achieving goals. This involves using appropriate language, avoiding misinterpretation, and considering the context and audience of the message. Mindful communication similarly emphasizes the importance of clear and effective communication and encourages the use of nonviolent communication techniques to minimize misunderstandings and promote mutual understanding.

- Open Communication: Enlightened heart leaders prioritize open communication, recognizing the importance of creating an environment where employees feel comfortable sharing their thoughts, opinions, and concerns. This involves creating channels for feedback, being receptive to criticism, and encouraging open dialogue. Mindful communication similarly emphasizes the importance of creating a safe and nonjudgmental space for communication and encourages the use of active listening and open-mindedness to foster mutual understanding and cooperation.

- Mindful Communication as a Tool for Conflict Resolution: Enlightened heart leaders recognize that conflicts may arise in the workplace and prioritize using mindful communication as a tool for conflict resolution. This involves approaching conflicts with empathy, seeking to understand the perspectives of all parties involved, and finding mutually beneficial solutions. Mindful communication similarly emphasizes the use of nonjudgmental listening and open-mindedness to resolve conflicts and encourages the use of collaborative problem-solving techniques to find mutually acceptable solutions.

Mindful communication is a key component of enlightened heart leadership, as both concepts prioritize clear, effective, and compassionate communication in promoting understanding, building trust, and creating a positive work environment. By practicing mindful communication techniques, enlightened heart leaders can create a culture of open communication, effective conflict resolution, and collaboration, ultimately leading to greater success and satisfaction in the workplace. Effective communication is a critical component of enlightened heart leadership.

In this chapter, we will explore the principles of mindful communication and how they can be applied in a leadership context. We will discuss the importance of active listening, speaking with intention, and communicating with empathy and compassion. Leadership requires a great deal of attention and focus, and yet many leaders find themselves distracted by the endless demands of their roles. Mindful leadership offers a solution to this challenge by emphasizing the importance of being present and attentive in every moment. We will explore the key principles of mindful leadership and how they can be applied in various leadership contexts. By practicing mindfulness, leaders can develop greater clarity, focus, and emotional intelligence, which can help them to make better decisions and communicate more effectively with their team members. The benefits of mindful leadership are numerous. By practicing mindfulness, leaders can develop greater self-awareness, which can help them to recognize their own limitations and biases. They can also become more attuned to the needs and perspectives of their team members, which can help them to build stronger relationships and foster a more positive work environment. In addition, mindful leaders tend to be more effective problem-solvers, as they are better able to remain calm and focused in the face of adversity.

There are many practical applications of mindful leadership in various leadership contexts. For example, leaders can practice mindfulness during meetings by staying fully present and engaged, listening actively to what others are saying, and avoiding distractions. They can also practice mindfulness during one-on-one conversations with team members by being fully present and attentive, asking open-ended questions, and avoiding assumptions or judgments. Another practical application of mindful leadership is to take time for self-reflection. By setting aside time each day to reflect on their thoughts and emotions, leaders can develop greater self-awareness and identify areas where they may need to improve. This can help them to become more effective leaders and build stronger relationships with their team members. Mindful leadership can also be applied to decision-making. By taking a mindful approach to decision-making, leaders can consider all relevant information, weigh the pros and cons of each option, and make decisions that are in the best interests of their team and organization. Mindful leadership is a powerful approach to leadership that emphasizes the importance of being fully present and aware in every moment. By practicing mindfulness, leaders can develop greater self-awareness, emotional intelligence, and clarity of thought, which can help them to make better decisions and communicate more effectively with their team members.

SUSTAINMENT

Someone with an enlightened heart approach to feedback would prioritize compassionate and effective communication, with the goal of helping employees grow and develop their skills while also fostering a positive and supportive work environment. The following are some key principles that someone with an enlightened heart approach to feedback might follow:

- Start with Positive Feedback: An enlightened heart leader would start with positive feedback to set a positive tone for the conversation. This might involve recognizing an employee's strengths, achievements, or contributions to the team and acknowledging the value they bring to the organization.

- Offer Specific and Constructive Feedback: Enlightened heart leaders would provide specific and constructive feedback that is focused on behaviors or actions rather than personality or character traits. They would avoid judgmental or critical language and instead focus on offering practical and actionable feedback that can help the employee improve.

- Use Empathetic and Compassionate Language: An enlightened heart leader would use empathetic and compassionate language when giving feedback, acknowledging the employee's feelings and experiences and expressing support and encouragement. They would avoid language that is confrontational or dismissive of the employee's perspective.

- Encourage Self-Reflection: An enlightened heart leader would encourage self-reflection and self-awareness in the employee, helping them to recognize their strengths and areas for improvement. They might ask questions that help the employee to reflect on their actions, identify their own strengths and weaknesses, and develop their own strategies for improvement.

- Offer Support and Resources: Finally, an enlightened heart leader would offer support and resources to help the employee grow and develop. This might involve providing additional training or coaching, connecting the employee with mentors or other resources, or offering feedback and support on an ongoing basis.

Our experiences and interactions are often indirect and from a distant physical interaction that would typically have fed all of our senses. Opportunities for feedback and assessments are now increasingly being replaced by virtual alternatives, including email, texting, and social networking. Thus, relationships are becoming increasingly defined by virtual interaction, which is illusionary and can distort and substitute reality. Part of the difficulty with virtual alternatives to life is that they increase the likely hood of trauma. This may sound odd, but keep in mind that newer trauma research is showing that a person does not have to go through a major traumatic event, such as a plane crash or severe child abuse, to be considered traumatized. We now understand that there are smaller-sized traumas that likely affect every person in the world. For example, when a person's reality is not acknowledged as "real" by a significant other, is now considered traumatizing. Understanding that trauma dramatically affects the way that our mind functions is critical to understanding why all these virtual interactions are confusing. People simply are unable to process information. Meaningful learning occurs when the person engages in three basic kinds of cognitive processes: selecting, organizing, and integrating. The basic hypothesis is that people seek to make sense of the world by building coherent mental representations. A building block of mental representations is called schema. A schema (singular) represents generic knowledge. A general category (schema) will include slots for all the components, or features, included in it. Schemata (plural) are embedded one within another at different levels of abstraction. Relationships among them are conceived to be like webs (rather than hierarchical); thus, each one is interconnected with many others. This web aspect of schema is critical to understanding our minds and therefore our lives.

The challenge here is that leaders seeking opportunities for feedback and assessments—because face-to-face modes of interaction are now increasingly being replaced by virtual alternatives, including email, texting, and social networking—need to process increasing schemata which draws additional mental resources (including time, emotional, and mental cognitions) resulting in the likelihood of missing aspects of reality. The implication here is that leaders must encourage people, problems, and variables from a myriad of directions within their interactions to create meaningful learning, while recognizing the distortion effect might be at play and plan for it. Leaders need to see that relationships between variables exist within a web, then be open and train themselves to traverse multiple directions in order to see (let alone solve) our business problems. An enlightened heart leader would approach feedback to employees with a focus on compassion, empathy, and constructive feedback that encourages growth and development. By following these principles, an enlightened heart leader can create a positive and supportive work environment that fosters personal and professional growth for all employees.

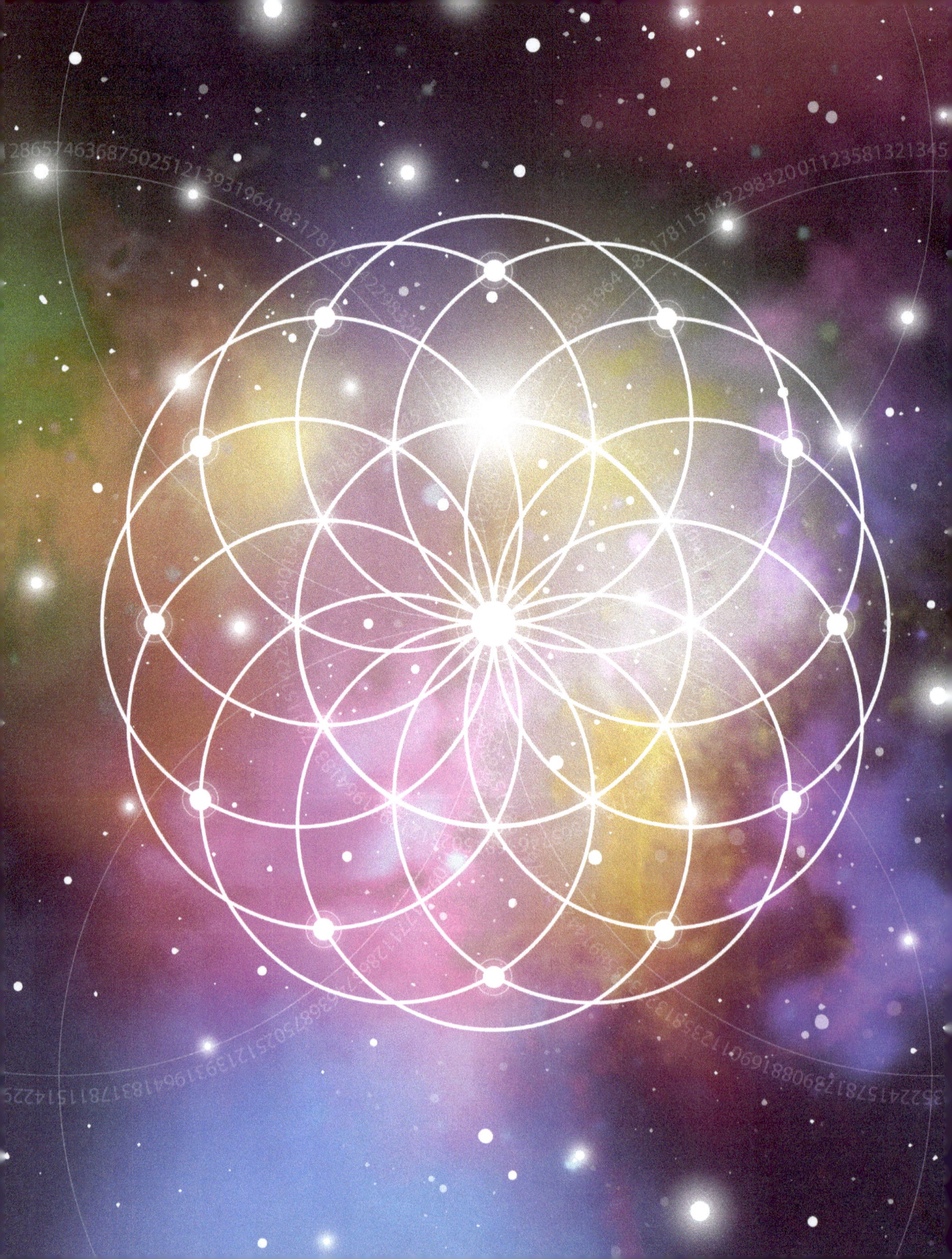

CHAPTER FOUR

Leading with Emotional Intelligence

"You must be at the end of the rope. I felt a tug."
— Author unknown

Emotional intelligence is an essential component of effective leadership. In this chapter, we will explore the role of emotional intelligence in enlightened heart leadership. We will discuss how leaders can develop their emotional intelligence skills and use them to build stronger relationships with their team members. We will also explore the importance of emotional self-regulation and how it can help leaders to make better decisions. Emotional intelligence is the ability to understand and manage one's own emotions, as well as the emotions of others. It is an essential skill for effective leadership, as it allows leaders to build strong relationships with their team members and to create a positive and supportive work environment. Here we will explore the relationship between enlightened heart leadership and emotional intelligence and how leaders can develop their emotional intelligence to become more

Illustration: Shutterstock

effective leaders. Emotional intelligence is essential for effective leadership because it allows leaders to connect with their team members on an emotional level. When leaders are able to understand and respond to their team members' emotions, they are more likely to build trust and respect. In addition, leaders with high emotional intelligence are better able to manage conflict, inspire their team members, and create a positive work environment.

ENLIGHTENED HEART LEADERSHIP AND EMOTIONAL INTELLIGENCE

Enlightened heart leadership emphasizes the importance of empathy, compassion, and self-awareness, all of which are key components of emotional intelligence. Leaders who practice enlightened heart leadership are able to connect with their team members on an emotional level, understand their needs and motivations, and respond with empathy and kindness.

Developing Emotional Intelligence

Emotional intelligence can be developed through self-reflection, practice, and feedback. Leaders can improve their emotional intelligence by:

- Developing Self-Awareness: Leaders can become more self-aware by reflecting on their own emotions, thoughts, and behaviors. This can involve keeping a journal, seeking feedback from others, or working with a coach or mentor.
- Practicing Empathy: Leaders can practice empathy by actively listening to their team members, trying to understand their perspectives, and responding with kindness and support.
- Managing Emotions: Leaders can develop their ability to manage their own emotions by learning to recognize and regulate their emotional responses. This can involve techniques such as mindfulness, meditation, or deep breathing exercises.
- Building Relationships: Leaders can build strong relationships with their team members by communicating effectively, showing respect and empathy, and being open to feedback.

Emotional intelligence is an essential skill for effective leadership, and it is closely aligned with the principles of enlightened heart leadership. By developing their emotional intelligence, leaders can build strong relationships with their team members, inspire loyalty and respect, and create a positive and supportive work environment.

CHAPTER FIVE

The Power of Self-Care and Intentional Healing

*"I go to nature to be soothed and healed,
and to have my senses put in order."*
— John Burroughs

Enlightened heart leadership recognizes the importance of healing, both individually and collectively, as a transformative force in creating a nurturing and compassionate organizational culture. In this chapter, we explore the concept of intentional healing and its profound connection to enlightened heart leadership. We delve into the role of healing in self-awareness, emotional intelligence, resilience, and fostering authentic connections within teams and organizations. By integrating intentional healing practices into their leadership approach, leaders can cultivate an environment that supports the holistic well-being and growth of individuals while fostering a culture of empathy, compassion, and positive transformation.

Illustration: Shutterstock

Healing Self

- Self-Awareness and Reflection: Intentional healing begins with self-awareness. Enlightened heart leaders engage in self-reflection and introspection to identify and heal their own emotional wounds, limiting beliefs, and past traumas. This process enables leaders to develop a deeper understanding of themselves, their triggers, and their patterns of behavior.
- Emotional Intelligence and Regulation: Healing enables leaders to cultivate emotional intelligence, which involves recognizing, understanding, and managing emotions. By healing emotional wounds, leaders develop the capacity to regulate their emotions effectively and respond to challenging situations with empathy, compassion, and wisdom.

Healing Relationships

- Empathy and Compassion: Intentional healing allows leaders to develop a heightened sense of empathy and compassion towards others. Leaders with an enlightened heart recognize the struggles and pain experienced by their team members and create a safe space for them to heal. They foster an environment where empathy and compassion are valued, leading to stronger and more authentic connections.
- Conflict Resolution and Forgiveness: Healing practices equip leaders with the skills to navigate conflicts and promote reconciliation. Leaders encourage open dialogue, active listening, and a willingness to understand different perspectives. By fostering an environment of forgiveness and reconciliation, leaders create a culture of trust and emotional well-being within their teams.

Healing Organizations

- Cultivating Psychological Safety: Enlightened heart leaders prioritize creating a psychologically safe environment where individuals feel comfortable expressing themselves, taking risks, and learning from mistakes. Healing practices help leaders identify and address any toxic behaviors, biases, or power dynamics that hinder a

culture of psychological safety.
- Supporting Holistic Well-Being: Leaders integrate intentional healing into organizational policies and practices, promoting the holistic well-being of their employees. This includes initiatives such as employee assistance programs, mindfulness practices, work-life balance support, and opportunities for personal and professional growth.

Resilience and Growth

- Building Resilience: Intentional healing contributes to the development of resilience in both leaders and teams. By acknowledging and healing past wounds, individuals and organizations can bounce back from adversity, adapt to change, and thrive in challenging situations. Leaders foster resilience by providing support, resources, and tools to help individuals navigate difficulties and grow stronger from their experiences.
- Continuous Learning and Growth: Healing practices encourage a growth mindset and a commitment to continuous learning. Enlightened heart leaders create opportunities for individuals to engage in personal and professional development, encouraging a culture of learning and growth within the organization.

Intentional healing plays a vital role in enlightened heart leadership, enabling leaders to heal themselves, nurture authentic relationships, and create thriving organizations. By engaging in intentional healing practices, leaders develop self-awareness, emotional intelligence, empathy, and resilience. They foster a culture of psychological safety, compassion, and growth, supporting the holistic well-being and growth of individuals within their teams and organizations.

As leaders integrate intentional healing into their leadership approach, they become catalysts for positive transformation, creating environments where individuals can heal, thrive, and contribute their best selves. May this chapter inspire leaders to embrace intentional healing as an integral part of enlightened heart leadership, ultimately fostering a more compassionate and flourishing organizational culture. A leader with an enlightened heart would approach intentional healing with compassion, empathy, and a deep commitment to creating a supportive and healing environment for all members of the team. The following are some key principles that a leader with an enlightened heart might follow when approaching intentional healing:

- Acknowledge and Address Trauma: An enlightened heart leader would acknowledge that members of the team may have experienced trauma and would work to create a safe and supportive environment for individuals to heal and recover. This might involve offering resources such as counseling or support groups or creating opportunities for team members to discuss their experiences and feelings in a safe and nonjudgmental environment.

- Foster a Culture of Compassion and Empathy: Enlightened heart leaders prioritize creating a culture of compassion and empathy, where team members are encouraged to support one another and offer help and understanding when needed. This might involve offering training in active listening and nonviolent communication or creating opportunities for team members to connect and build relationships outside of work.

- Encourage Self-Care: An enlightened heart leader would encourage team members to prioritize self-care, recognizing that taking care of oneself is a critical component of healing and recovery. This might involve offering resources such as yoga or meditation classes or encouraging team members to take time off or use flexible work arrangements when needed.

- Practice Humility and Vulnerability: An enlightened heart leader would practice humility and vulnerability, recognizing that they too may have experienced trauma or may be struggling with their own challenges. By modeling vulnerability and openness, the leader can create a culture where team members feel comfortable sharing their own experiences and seeking support.

- Foster a Sense of Purpose and Meaning: Finally, an enlightened heart leader would work to foster a sense of purpose and meaning for team members, helping them to connect with a sense of meaning and purpose that goes beyond their day-to-day work. This might involve offering opportunities for community service or volunteer work or connecting team members with causes or organizations that align with their values.

A leader with an enlightened heart would approach intentional healing with a deep commitment to creating a supportive and healing environment for all members of the team. By fostering a culture of compassion, empathy, and purpose, the leader can create a workplace where team members feel supported, valued, and empowered to heal and grow. In order to be effective leaders, it is important for individuals to take care of their own well-being. In this chapter, we will explore the importance of self-care in enlightened heart leadership and how leaders can incorporate self-care practices into their daily routines. We will discuss various strategies that leaders can use to maintain their physical, emotional, and mental well-being. Self-care is the practice of taking care of one's physical, mental, and emotional health. In the context of leadership, self-care is essential for maintaining energy, focus, and resilience in the face of challenges and stress.

THE IMPORTANCE OF SELF-CARE IN LEADERSHIP

Leaders who prioritize self-care are more likely to be effective in their roles. When leaders take care of their own physical, mental, and emotional health, they are better able to manage stress, make clear decisions, and maintain a positive attitude. In addition, leaders who practice self-care are more likely to model healthy behaviors for their team members, creating a culture of wellness and balance in the workplace. Enlightened heart leadership emphasizes the importance of compassion, empathy, and self-awareness, all of which are closely tied to self-care. Leaders who practice enlightened heart leadership recognize that self-care is essential for maintaining a sense of balance and well-being, and for building strong, sustainable relationships with team members.

Incorporating Self-Care Practices into Daily Life

There are many different self-care practices that leaders can incorporate into their daily routines. Some examples include:

- Prioritizing Sleep: Leaders should make sure to get enough sleep each night to ensure they are well-rested and able to focus during the day.
- Eating Well: Leaders should aim to eat a balanced diet that includes plenty of whole

foods and avoid processed and sugary foods.

- Exercising Regularly: Leaders should make time for regular exercise, whether that's through a structured workout routine or simply taking a walk during a break in the day.
- Practicing Mindfulness: Leaders can practice mindfulness through meditation, yoga, or other techniques that help them stay present and focused.
- Taking Breaks: Leaders should make sure to take regular breaks throughout the day to recharge and avoid burnout.

DESTRUCTION

While the notion of destruction may seem counterintuitive to enlightened heart leadership, there is a profound role it plays in the process of transformation and growth. In this article, we explore the concept of destruction and its significance in the context of enlightened heart leadership. We delve into how the intentional dismantling of outdated systems, beliefs, and structures can create space for innovation, authenticity, and positive change. By understanding and embracing the role of destruction, leaders can navigate the complexities of transformation with wisdom, compassion, and a vision for a better future. Enlightened heart leadership is often associated with qualities such as compassion, empathy, and the nurturing of positive change. It emphasizes the importance of fostering a harmonious and supportive environment for individuals and organizations to thrive. However, there is an often-overlooked aspect of enlightened heart leadership that deserves attention: the role of destruction.

Destruction, at first glance, evokes images of chaos, loss, and upheaval. However, when viewed through the lens of transformation and growth, destruction takes on a profound significance. At the heart of enlightened leadership lies the recognition that certain aspects of the status quo may no longer serve the best interests of individuals, teams, or organizations. It is an understanding that clinging to outdated practices, rigid structures, and limiting beliefs stifles growth and inhibits the emergence of new possibilities. In such cases, destruction becomes an essential catalyst for transformation and evolution. Destruction in enlightened heart leadership is not about mindless demolition or tearing down everything in its path. It is a deliberate and intentional process of letting go, questioning, and challenging existing norms, structures, and ways of thinking. It involves a courageous examination of what is no longer working and the willingness to embrace the unknown.

One aspect of destruction within enlightened heart leadership involves breaking limiting patterns. It requires leaders to identify outdated systems and practices that hinder growth, creativity, and collaboration. This may involve questioning long-standing traditions, hierarchical structures, and conventional wisdom. By dismantling these patterns, leaders create space for new ideas, fresh perspectives, and innovative approaches to emerge. Embracing destruction also requires leaders to navigate uncertainty with grace and resilience. It entails letting go of attachments to the familiar and embracing the possibilities that lie beyond the comfort zone.

This mindset of nonattachment allows leaders and their teams to adapt and respond effectively to changing circumstances and emerging trends. By embracing the concept of creative destruction, leaders understand that through the dismantling of old structures, there is an opportunity for innovative and sustainable growth. While destruction may seem disruptive, enlightened heart leaders approach it with empathy and compassion. They acknowledge the impact of change on individuals within the organization and actively address their concerns and needs. By communicating openly, providing support, and guiding their teams through the process of transformation, leaders create an environment that fosters resilience and growth.

However, destruction in enlightened heart leadership is not about tearing down without consideration. It is about consciously dismantling while simultaneously building bridges to new possibilities. Leaders create a vision for the future and engage stakeholders in co-creating the path forward. They cultivate an environment of trust, collaboration, and shared ownership, enabling the emergence of innovative ideas and collaborative solutions. Moreover, destruction within enlightened heart leadership is not solely focused on external structures and systems. It also involves the dismantling of internal barriers and masks that hinder authenticity and genuine connections. Enlightened heart leaders create a safe and inclusive space where individuals can shed their masks, express their true selves, and engage in open and honest dialogue. This process cultivates an environment where vulnerability is celebrated, fostering deeper relationships and meaningful connections.

The role of destruction in enlightened heart leadership should not be underestimated. It is an essential element in the journey of transformation, growth, and positive change. By intentionally dismantling outdated systems, beliefs, and structures, leaders create space for innovation, authenticity, and new possibilities to flourish. Through destruction, enlightened heart leaders challenge the status quo, navigate uncertainty with resilience, and foster environments that support the holistic well-being and growth of individuals and organizations. Together, let us embrace the power of destruction as a catalyst for growth and create a world where enlightened heart leadership paves the way for a brighter and more sustainable future.

Breaking Limiting Patterns

- Identifying Outdated Systems: Enlightened heart leaders recognize the need to identify and dismantle outdated systems and practices that no longer serve the organization or its stakeholders. This includes questioning long-standing traditions, beliefs, and processes to foster an environment that is open to new possibilities.

- Challenging Status Quo: Leaders who embrace destruction challenge the status quo and encourage their teams to do the same. They create a culture where individuals feel empowered to voice their concerns, challenge existing norms, and explore innovative solutions that lead to positive change.

Embracing Uncertainty

- Letting Go of Attachments: Destruction in enlightened heart leadership involves letting go of attachments to outdated ways of thinking, being, and doing. Leaders cultivate a mindset of nonattachment, allowing space for new ideas, perspectives, and approaches to emerge.

- Embracing Creative Destruction: Leaders embrace the concept of creative destruction, understanding that through the dismantling of old structures, there is an opportunity for innovative and sustainable growth. They foster an environment that encourages experimentation, learning from failures, and adapting to emerging trends.

Compassionate Transformation

- Acknowledging the Impact: Enlightened heart leaders approach destruction with empathy and compassion, recognizing that change can be disruptive and create uncertainty for individuals within the organization. They communicate openly, provide support, and guide their teams through the process of transformation.
- Building Bridges: Again, recall that destruction in enlightened heart leadership is not about tearing down without consideration. It is about consciously dismantling while simultaneously building bridges to new possibilities. Leaders create a vision for the future and engage stakeholders in co-creating the path forward.

Creating Space for Authenticity

- Removing Masks and Barriers: Destruction involves removing the masks and barriers that hinder authenticity within individuals and the organization. Enlightened heart leaders create a safe and inclusive space where individuals can express their true selves, fostering an environment that encourages vulnerability, honesty, and genuine connections.
- Cultivating Trust and Collaboration: Through destruction, leaders create opportunities for individuals and teams to come together, collaborate, and build trust. They foster a culture of open communication, active listening, and shared ownership, enabling the emergence of innovative ideas and collaborative solutions.

Destruction, when approached with an enlightened heart, plays a crucial role in the process of transformation and growth within organizations. Enlightened heart leaders understand that dismantling outdated systems, beliefs, and structures is necessary to create space for innovation, authenticity, and positive change. By embracing destruction, leaders challenge the status quo, foster an environment of openness and creativity, and navigate the complexities of transformation with wisdom and compassion. Through this process, leaders create an organizational culture that values continuous improvement, adaptability, and the collective well-being of all stakeholders. May this chapter inspire leaders to embrace the role of destruction in enlightened heart leadership, leading their organizations towards a future that is rooted in authenticity, innovation, and positive transformation.

The process of creation, preservation, and destruction is seen as a natural and necessary cycle of life. The god Brahma is responsible for creating the universe, Vishnu is responsible for preserving it, and Shiva is responsible for destroying it in order to make way for new creation. This cycle is seen as an essential part of the cosmic order, and is thought to be mirrored in all aspects of human life, including leadership and organizations. Enlightened heart leaders understand that change is inevitable, and that in order to grow and evolve, it is often necessary to let go of old patterns, beliefs, and behaviors that are no longer serving the higher good. This process of letting go can be difficult and uncomfortable but is also necessary for progress. The role of destruction in enlightened heart leadership is therefore seen as a transformative process that leads to growth, evolution, and renewal. This may involve letting go of old practices or ways of thinking that are hindering progress, or making difficult decisions that may be unpopular in the short term but serve the best interests of the team and the organization in the long term. However, it is important to note that the process of destruction should be approached with mindfulness, wisdom, and a deep commitment to the well-being of all members of the team. The principles of Dharma (righteousness) and karma (action and consequence) guide individuals and leaders to act with integrity and responsibility. Enlightened heart leaders understand that the process of destruction can be painful and disruptive, and strive to approach it with compassion, empathy, and a deep commitment to the well-being of all members of the team. They work to create a supportive environment where team members feel heard, valued, and empowered to participate in the process of change and transformation.

Ultimately, the role of destruction in enlightened heart leadership is to create space for new ideas, practices, and ways of being that are aligned with the higher good and serve the best interests of the team and the organization. By approaching the process of destruction with wisdom, mindfulness, and compassion, enlightened heart leaders can guide their teams through periods of change and transformation, and create a culture of growth, evolution, and renewal.

The concept of organic growth in leadership raises the question of whether personal and professional development can occur without intentional effort. While socialization and learning from others can contribute to organic growth, intentional effort can accelerate it. This suggests that we can teach accelerated growth in leadership. However, it's important to recognize that everything we interact with, including people and our environment, influences our learning and development. As such, intentional healing and learning can be powerful tools for achieving accelerated growth and development in leadership. As Emmet Fox writes in *Sermon on the Mount*, "Nothing can come into our experience unless it finds something in us with which it is attuned" (p. 45). For us, what that means is a person cannot work on something they do not yet notice. As a leader, achieving accelerated growth in development of leadership will need to include intentionally requesting, listening to, and taking in meaningful feedback. We may not think so, but most everyone (if not everyone) thinks that they "know" themselves, each other, and of course, reality. Just ask any person a simple question like "how's it going?" and they'll respond with a narrative about their life—meaning how their particular life is going from their own specific perspective. Now, if you notice that one or two of the thoughts that they share are not true, or perhaps slightly off, you can push against it and maybe come out of the conversation unscathed, and maybe not. Turns out that people aren't keen on holes being poked in their sense of self or reality.

Simple but not easy; a price will have to be paid, and that price is certainty in knowing. Give it up and embrace instead the not-knowing perspective. If someone points out a seemingly negative aspect of your leadership, search your experience for where it might be true and work on it in your professional development. This will accelerate your growth as a leader.

Self-care is an essential component of enlightened heart leadership. By prioritizing their own physical, mental, and emotional well-being, leaders can maintain a sense of balance and resilience in the face of challenges and stress. In addition, leaders who practice self-care are more likely to model healthy behaviors for their team members, creating a culture of wellness and balance in the workplace. In the following chapters, we will explore other key principles of enlightened heart leadership and how they can be applied in various leadership contexts.

THE ROLE OF CHANGE WITHIN ENLIGHTENED HEART LEADERSHIP

Change is an inherent and constant aspect of life and organizations. In the context of enlightened leadership, the ability to understand and navigate change is vital. Enlightened leaders recognize that change is not merely a disruption or an obstacle to be overcome but an opportunity for growth, transformation, and positive impact. Change is an inevitable part of life and organizations. In the dynamic and rapidly evolving world we live in, the ability to understand and navigate change is not only important but vital for leaders who aspire to practice enlightened leadership. Enlightened leaders recognize that change is not something to be feared or resisted, but rather a powerful force that can catalyze growth, transformation, and positive impact. In this chapter, we delve into the profound significance of understanding the role of change in enlightened leadership and explore how leaders can embrace change to create thriving and resilient organizations.

Change, in its essence, is a process of transitioning from one state to another. It can manifest in various forms, such as technological advancements, market disruptions, shifts in customer preferences, or internal organizational transformations. For enlightened leaders, change is not seen as a disruption or a hindrance, but rather as an opportunity for progress, innovation, and personal and collective development. Enlightened leaders recognize the inherent value of embracing change and the positive impact it can have on individuals, teams, and organizations. They understand that change is not an isolated event but a continuous and ongoing process. By cultivating a mindset that embraces change as a natural and necessary part of growth, enlightened leaders inspire their teams to adopt a similar perspective, creating a culture that embraces adaptability, resilience, and continuous improvement. One of the fundamental reasons understanding the role of change is vital in enlightened leadership is because it fosters a culture of continuous improvement. Enlightened leaders recognize that standing still is not an option in today's fast-paced and competitive business environment. They encourage their teams to embrace change as a means of learning, innovation, and staying ahead of the curve. By instilling a mindset of continuous improvement, leaders create an organizational culture that values creativity, curiosity, and a commitment to ongoing development.

Navigating complexity and uncertainty is another key reason why understanding the role of change is crucial in enlightened leadership. The world we live in is characterized by rapid technological advancements, disruptive market forces, and unpredictable external factors. Enlightened leaders recognize the need to navigate these complexities with agility and resilience. They understand that change often brings uncertainty and ambiguity, and they are adept at guiding their teams through these challenging times. By embracing change and leading with clarity and confidence, enlightened leaders inspire trust and build a resilient and adaptable organizational culture.

Enlightened leaders also play a pivotal role in facilitating organizational transformation.

They recognize that in order to remain relevant and thrive in a constantly evolving landscape, organizations must be open to change and willing to challenge existing structures, processes, and mindsets. They proactively initiate and lead transformative initiatives, fostering an environment where change is seen as an opportunity for growth and positive evolution. By championing change, enlightened leaders empower their teams to embrace new ways of thinking, embrace innovative practices, and contribute to the organization's continuous development and success. Furthermore, understanding the role of change is essential in fostering innovation and creativity within an organization. Change often disrupts the status quo and challenges existing paradigms. Enlightened leaders create a culture that encourages exploration, experimentation, and the pursuit of new ideas. They understand that by embracing change, individuals and teams are more likely to think outside the box, challenge conventional thinking, and come up with innovative solutions to complex problems. By providing the necessary resources, support, and autonomy, enlightened leaders create an environment where innovation can flourish, leading to competitive advantage and sustainable growth.

Change, when managed effectively, can have a profound impact on employee engagement and well-being. Enlightened leaders recognize the importance of involving employees in the change process and ensuring their voices are heard and valued. They communicate transparently, provide clarity, and support their teams during times of change. By involving employees in decision-making processes, leaders tap into their unique perspectives, talents, and insights, fostering a sense of ownership, empowerment, and personal growth. In turn, this leads to increased employee engagement, enhanced well-being, and a stronger sense of purpose and satisfaction.

Enlightened leaders also understand that change is closely linked to learning and growth. Change provides opportunities for individuals and organizations to learn, adapt, and evolve. Leaders who understand the role of change foster a culture of continuous learning, where ongoing development is valued and integrated into the fabric of the organization. They create learning opportunities, encourage experimentation, and promote a growth mindset among their teams. By embracing change as a catalyst for learning, leaders inspire curiosity, resilience, and a commitment to personal and professional growth. Understanding the role of change is vital in enlightened leadership. By embracing change as a catalyst for growth, innovation, and transformation, leaders create resilient, adaptable, and thriving organizations. They navigate complexity with grace, foster a culture of continuous improvement, and empower individuals to embrace change as an opportunity for learning and personal growth.

As leaders embrace the role of change, they become catalysts for positive transformation, creating organizations that are agile, forward-thinking, and capable of making a meaningful impact in an ever-changing world. May this chapter inspire leaders to recognize and embrace the power of change and its potential to unlock new possibilities and create a brighter future for themselves and their organizations.

In the following section, we explore why understanding the role of change is crucial in enlightened leadership and how leaders can embrace change to create thriving and resilient organizations.

- Embracing Continuous Improvement: Enlightened leaders understand that change is synonymous with progress. They foster a culture of continuous improvement, encouraging individuals and teams to embrace change as a means of learning, innovation, and staying ahead in a rapidly evolving world. By embracing change, leaders inspire a growth mindset, adaptability, and a commitment to ongoing development.

- Navigating Complexity and Uncertainty: In today's complex and unpredictable business landscape, leaders who understand the role of change are better equipped to navigate uncertainty. They anticipate and respond to external disruptions, technological advancements, and market shifts with agility and resilience. By embracing change, leaders inspire confidence and trust in their teams, fostering an environment that is adaptable and capable of thriving amidst uncertainty.

- Facilitating Organizational Transformation: Change often involves transformation on an organizational level. Enlightened leaders recognize the need to challenge traditional structures, processes, and mindsets that may hinder growth and progress. They proactively initiate and lead transformative initiatives, empowering their teams to embrace change, overcome resistance, and contribute to the organization's evolution.

- Fostering Innovation and Creativity: Change is closely intertwined with innovation and creativity. Enlightened leaders create a culture that encourages exploration, experimentation, and the pursuit of new ideas. By understanding the role of change, leaders foster an environment where individuals feel safe to take risks, learn from failures, and think outside the box. They provide the necessary resources, support, and autonomy for innovation to thrive.

- Enhancing Employee Engagement and Well-Being: Change, when managed effectively, can have a positive impact on employee engagement and well-being. Enlightened leaders communicate transparently, involve employees in decision-making processes, and provide clarity and support during times of change. By involving employees in the change process, leaders tap into their unique perspectives, talents, and insights, fostering a sense of ownership, empowerment, and personal growth.
- Nurturing a Learning Organization: Change is closely linked to learning and growth. Enlightened leaders view change as an opportunity for individuals and organizations to learn, adapt, and evolve. They create a learning culture where continuous learning and development are valued and integrated into the fabric of the organization. By understanding the role of change in fostering learning, leaders inspire curiosity, resilience, and a commitment to personal and professional growth.

Understanding the role of change is vital in enlightened leadership. By embracing change as a catalyst for growth, innovation, and transformation, leaders create resilient, adaptable, and thriving organizations. They navigate complexity with grace, foster a culture of continuous improvement, and empower individuals to embrace change as an opportunity for learning and personal growth. As leaders embrace the role of change, they become catalysts for positive transformation, creating organizations that are agile, forward-thinking, and capable of making a meaningful impact in an ever-changing world.

Change is a central aspect of enlightened heart leadership. An enlightened heart leader is someone who is committed to creating positive change in their organization, their team, and the world around them. They are guided by a deep sense of purpose and a strong desire to make a meaningful difference in the lives of others. The role of change in enlightened heart leadership can be understood in several ways. First, enlightened heart leaders recognize that change is inevitable and necessary for growth and evolution. They understand that organizations and teams must adapt to changing circumstances and shifting priorities in order to remain relevant and effective. Second, enlightened heart leaders view change as an opportunity to create a better future for their team and their organization. They approach change with a vision for what is possible, and work to inspire their team to embrace new ideas, practices, and ways of working. Third, enlightened heart leaders recognize that change can be difficult and uncomfortable and strive to create a supportive environment where team members feel safe to express their concerns, fears, and hopes for the future. They work to build trust and open communication channels with their team and seek to involve them in the process of change and transformation. Fourth, enlightened heart leaders understand that change is not a one-time event but an ongoing process of growth and evolution. They are committed to continuous learning and improvement, and strive to create a culture of innovation, experimentation, and risk-taking. Finally, enlightened heart leaders view change as an opportunity to create a more compassionate and just world. They are committed to promoting social and environmental sustainability, and work to align their organization's goals and values with the greater good. In short, the role of change in enlightened heart leadership is to create a culture of growth, evolution, and renewal and to use change as a means to create a more positive and compassionate world.

Enlightened heart leaders approach change management in a different way compared to traditional approaches. They recognize that change can be difficult and uncomfortable for team members and are aware that simply imposing change from the top down may not be effective.

Here are some ways in which enlightened heart leaders approach change management differently:

- Emphasis on Empathy and Compassion: Enlightened heart leaders prioritize empathy and compassion when managing change. They seek to understand the concerns, fears, and hopes of their team members and work to create a supportive environment where team members feel safe to express themselves. They recognize that change can be stressful, and take steps to alleviate the anxiety and uncertainty that may arise during the change process.
- Collaboration and Participation: Enlightened heart leaders involve team members in the change process, seeking their input and ideas on how to best manage the

change. They understand that team members often have valuable insights and perspectives that can help inform the change process. By involving team members in the change process, they create a sense of ownership and engagement, which can lead to better outcomes.

- Vision and Purpose: Enlightened heart leaders articulate a clear vision and purpose for the change process, helping team members to understand the goals and objectives of the change. They communicate the benefits of the change and explain how it will contribute to the organization's overall mission and values. By connecting the change to a higher purpose, they create a sense of meaning and motivation for team members.

- Flexibility and Adaptability: Enlightened heart leaders recognize that change can be unpredictable and that plans may need to be adjusted as circumstances evolve. They are flexible and adaptable, willing to make adjustments as needed to ensure the success of the change process. They work to create a culture of experimentation and innovation, where team members are encouraged to try new approaches and learn from their experiences.

- Continuous Learning and Improvement: Enlightened heart leaders approach change management as an ongoing process of learning and improvement. They seek feedback from team members and other stakeholders, using this feedback to refine their approach and make adjustments as needed. They are committed to continuous improvement and strive to create a culture of learning and growth.

Enlightened heart leaders approach change management with empathy, collaboration, and a clear sense of purpose. They involve team members in the process, create a supportive environment, and are flexible and adaptable in their approach. By prioritizing the needs of their team members and working to create a culture of learning and growth, they are able to manage change in a way that promotes positive outcomes and long-term success.

CHAPTER SIX

Navigating Challenging Situations

"When we are motivated by goals that have deep meaning, by dreams that need completion, by pure love that needs expressing, then we truly live life."
— Greg Anderson

Enlightened heart leaders are individuals who lead with compassion, empathy, and a deep understanding of human nature. They prioritize the well-being of their team members and seek to create an environment where everyone feels safe, supported, and valued. However, even with the best intentions, challenging situations may arise in the workplace that require careful navigation. In this essay, we will explore how enlightened heart leaders navigate challenging situations and the key principles that guide their approach.

- Mindfulness and Self-Awareness: Enlightened heart leaders prioritize mindfulness and self-awareness as key tools for navigating challenging situations. They recognize

Illustration: Shutterstock

that their own emotions and biases may impact their decision-making and seek to cultivate a deeper understanding of themselves and their reactions. By remaining mindful and self-aware, they are better able to manage their own emotions and respond in a calm, measured way to difficult situations.

- Compassion and Empathy: Compassion and empathy are central to enlightened heart leadership and are key in navigating challenging situations. Enlightened heart leaders seek to understand the perspectives and feelings of all parties involved and work to find solutions that are in the best interest of everyone. By approaching challenging situations with compassion and empathy, they are better able to build trust and create a supportive environment where everyone feels heard and valued.

- Communication and Transparency: Communication and transparency are critical for navigating challenging situations. Enlightened heart leaders prioritize open and honest communication with all stakeholders, sharing information and feedback in a timely and respectful manner. They seek to build trust and credibility with their team members and are transparent about their decision-making process. By fostering a culture of open communication, they are able to minimize misunderstandings and build a strong foundation for navigating challenging situations.

- Collaboration and Teamwork: Enlightened heart leaders recognize the value of collaboration and teamwork in navigating challenging situations. They seek to involve all stakeholders in the decision-making process, soliciting feedback and input from team members, customers, and other stakeholders. They work to build a strong team culture, where everyone feels valued and supported, and are committed to finding solutions that are in the best interest of the team as a whole.

- Creativity and Innovation: Finally, enlightened heart leaders are creative and innovative in their approach to navigating challenging situations. They seek to find new and innovative solutions that may not have been considered before and are willing to take calculated risks to achieve their goals. They foster a culture of experimentation and learning where team members are encouraged to try new approaches and learn from their experiences.

Enlightened heart leaders navigate challenging situations with mindfulness, compassion, communication, collaboration, and creativity. By prioritizing the well-being of their team members, seeking to understand different perspectives, and working to build a culture of trust and transparency, they are able to successfully navigate even the most difficult situations.

Leadership is not always easy, and leaders will inevitably face difficult situations from time to time. In this chapter, we will explore how leaders can navigate challenging situations with compassion and mindfulness. We will discuss the importance of staying calm under pressure and how leaders can use their emotional intelligence skills to find creative solutions to problems.

Leadership can be a challenging role, and there are often situations that require leaders to navigate difficult and complex circumstances. In these moments, it can be easy to fall back on old habits or default to an authoritarian leadership style. However, with an enlightened heart approach, leaders can navigate challenging situations with greater empathy, compassion, and wisdom. We will explore how leaders can use an enlightened heart approach to navigate challenging situations and build stronger relationships with their team members. Challenging situations can come in many forms, from conflicts between team members to unexpected changes in the business environment. Whatever the situation may be, it's important for leaders to approach it with an open mind and a willingness to listen to different perspectives. By doing so, leaders can gain a deeper understanding of the situation and the underlying causes, which can help them to identify the best course of action.

APPLYING ENLIGHTENED HEART PRINCIPLES

Enlightened heart leadership is a leadership approach that prioritizes compassion, empathy, and mindfulness. At its core, it is a way of leading that seeks to create a positive, supportive environment where individuals feel valued, heard, and supported. There are several core principles that guide enlightened heart leadership:

- Compassion and Empathy: Compassion and empathy are central to enlightened heart leadership. Leaders who embrace this approach seek to understand the perspectives and feelings of others and work to create an environment where everyone feels heard, valued, and supported.

- Mindfulness: Mindfulness is another key principle of enlightened heart leadership. Leaders who embrace this approach seek to remain present and engaged in the moment, paying attention to their own thoughts and emotions as well as those of others. They strive to remain calm, centered, and focused, even in the face of challenging situations.

- Collaboration and Teamwork: Enlightened heart leaders recognize that collaboration and teamwork are critical to success. They seek to build strong teams where everyone feels valued and supported and work to foster a culture of open communication and collaboration.

- Creativity and Innovation: Enlightened heart leaders are creative and innovative in their approach to problem-solving. They are willing to take risks and try new approaches to achieve their goals, and they encourage their team members to do the same.

- Integrity and Ethics: Finally, enlightened heart leaders are committed to integrity and ethics. They prioritize honesty, transparency, and fairness in all of their interactions and decisions and seek to build a culture of trust and accountability.

By embracing these core principles, enlightened heart leaders are able to create a positive, supportive environment where everyone feels valued, heard, and supported. They are able to lead with compassion, empathy, and mindfulness and are committed to building strong teams and finding innovative solutions to the challenges they face.

An enlightened heart approach to leadership involves cultivating qualities such as empathy, compassion, and self-awareness. When applied to challenging situations, these principles can help leaders to:

- Listen Deeply: By listening carefully to team members' concerns, leaders can gain a better understanding of the situation and build trust with their team.

- Communicate Effectively: Clear and empathetic communication can help to defuse tense situations and find common ground.

- Practice Empathy: Leaders who put themselves in their team members' shoes are

better able to understand their perspective and find mutually beneficial solutions.
- Be Self-Aware: Leaders who are aware of their own biases and emotions can make better decisions and avoid letting their own emotions cloud their judgment.
- Cultivate Compassion: Compassion for team members who may be struggling can help to build stronger relationships and create a more supportive workplace culture.

NAVIGATING CONFLICT

Conflict is an inherent part of human interaction, and within the context of leadership, it often arises as a result of differing perspectives, goals, and interests. Traditional approaches to conflict resolution often prioritize power dynamics or compromise, seeking to achieve a resolution that may leave underlying tensions unresolved. However, enlightened heart leaders approach conflict with a different mindset—one rooted in compassion, understanding, and a deep appreciation for the well-being of all individuals involved. Enlightened heart leadership acknowledges that conflict, when approached with an open mind and heart, can become a transformative opportunity for growth, understanding, and improved relationships. It recognizes that conflict, when properly managed, can lead to innovative solutions, strengthened team dynamics, and personal development. Thus, the aim of this chapter is to explore how leaders with enlightened hearts navigate conflict, foster constructive dialogue, and facilitate resolution that honors the values of empathy, respect, and growth.

Embracing Conflict as an Opportunity for Growth

Enlightened heart leaders fundamentally shift their perspective on conflict, viewing it as an inherent part of human relationships and organizational dynamics. Instead of fearing or avoiding conflict, they embrace it as an opportunity for growth and learning. They recognize that conflict, when approached with openness and curiosity, can uncover underlying issues, challenge assumptions, and generate creative solutions. By reframing conflict as a catalyst for positive change, enlightened leaders create a culture where conflicts are seen as constructive and valuable.

Cultivating Emotional Intelligence

Leaders with enlightened hearts understand the importance of emotional intelligence in effectively navigating conflict. Emotional intelligence encompasses self-awareness, self-regulation, empathy, and social skills. By developing these qualities, leaders can better understand their own emotions, manage their reactions, and empathize with the emotions of others involved in the conflict. Emotional intelligence enables leaders to approach conflict with composure, patience, and a genuine desire to understand different perspectives.

Active Listening and Empathic Understanding

Enlightened heart leaders prioritize active listening and empathic understanding as essential tools for conflict resolution. They create a safe and nonjudgmental space where individuals feel heard and understood. Through active listening, leaders demonstrate genuine curiosity and seek to comprehend the underlying needs, values, and emotions driving the conflict. By empathically understanding the experiences and viewpoints of others, leaders can forge a deeper connection, build trust, and facilitate a more meaningful resolution.

Collaboration and Win-Win Solutions

Enlightened heart leaders reject the notion of conflict as a win-lose situation and instead foster a collaborative approach to resolution. They emphasize the importance of seeking win-win solutions that address the needs and interests of all parties involved. By promoting collaboration, they encourage individuals to work together, share perspectives, and co-create innovative solutions. Through constructive dialogue and a focus on shared objectives, enlightened leaders nurture an environment where conflicts can be resolved in ways that honor the values of empathy, respect, and mutual growth.

Mediation and Facilitation

In situations where conflicts involve multiple parties or complex dynamics, enlightened heart leaders may act as mediators or facilitators. They guide the process of conflict resolution, ensuring that all voices are heard and respected. They remain neutral, objective, and nonjudgmental, creating a safe and inclusive space for individuals to express their concerns.

Through skillful facilitation, enlightened leaders help parties find common ground, explore alternative perspectives, and work towards mutually acceptable solutions.

Restorative Justice and Healing

Enlightened heart leaders recognize that conflicts can cause harm, damage relationships, and create a sense of disconnection within the organization. They approach conflict resolution from a restorative justice perspective, seeking to address the root causes of the conflict and promote healing. They encourage individuals to take responsibility for their actions, engage in open dialogue, and actively work towards rebuilding trust and repairing relationships. By embracing restorative justice principles, enlightened leaders create an environment where conflicts can be resolved in a way that promotes understanding, growth, and the restoration of harmony.

Conflict is an inherent aspect of human relationships and organizational dynamics, but enlightened heart leaders approach conflict resolution with a unique perspective. By embracing conflict as an opportunity for growth, cultivating emotional intelligence, practicing active listening and empathy, promoting collaboration, and facilitating dialogue, leaders with enlightened hearts create an environment where conflicts are transformed into catalysts for positive change. They prioritize understanding, empathy, and the well-being of all individuals involved, working towards win-win solutions that honor the values of respect, compassion, and growth. In the chapters that follow, we will explore specific strategies and practices that enable leaders to navigate conflicts with an enlightened heart, fostering a culture of understanding and growth within their organizations.

PSEUDO SELF

In the realm of leadership, the concept of authenticity holds significant importance. Authentic leaders are those who lead with sincerity, integrity, and a genuine sense of self. They are individuals who are not afraid to be vulnerable, who embrace their strengths and weaknesses, and who inspire and motivate others through their genuine presence. However, in today's complex and demanding world, leaders often find themselves facing the challenge of maintaining their authentic selves while navigating various roles, expectations, and pressures.

This essay explores the concept of the pseudo self and its impact on enlightened heart leadership. We delve into the intricacies of the pseudo self, how it can manifest in leadership, and how enlightened leaders can cultivate authenticity and lead from their true selves.

Understanding the Pseudo Self

The pseudo self refers to a constructed identity that individuals create to fit societal expectations, norms, and roles. It is a self that is shaped by external influences, such as cultural conditioning, societal pressures, and organizational expectations. The pseudo self often emerges as a defense mechanism, protecting individuals from vulnerability and judgment. It is the self that individuals present to the world, often driven by the need for acceptance, validation, and success. While the pseudo self may serve as a temporary coping strategy, it can hinder authentic connection, self-expression, and true leadership.

The pseudo self arises from the belief that one's authentic self is not enough or may not be accepted by others. It can manifest in various ways, such as wearing masks to fit in, suppressing true emotions and desires, and conforming to societal or organizational norms that may contradict one's core values. The pseudo self is a constructed façade that individuals project, hiding their true thoughts, feelings, and aspirations behind a carefully curated image. It can be a result of societal conditioning, parental expectations, fear of rejection, or the desire to maintain a sense of control in a chaotic world.

The Dangers of the Pseudo Self in Leadership

When leaders operate from a place of the pseudo self, they may lose touch with their true values, passions, and purpose. They become disconnected from their authentic selves, leading to a lack of congruence between their inner being and their outward actions. The pseudo self can contribute to a sense of emptiness, disengagement, and a lack of fulfillment. Inauthentic leaders may find themselves constantly seeking external validation and approval, always striving to meet the expectations of others rather than leading from their core essence.

The pseudo self can also have detrimental effects on relationships within the organizational context. When leaders present a false image, it creates a sense of mistrust and disconnect among their teams. Individuals sense inauthenticity and may hesitate to fully engage, share their ideas, or express their concerns. The lack of trust inhibits collaboration, innovation, and open communication, hindering the overall growth and success of the organization.

Furthermore, the constant effort to maintain the pseudo self can lead to burnout. Leaders exhaust themselves trying to meet external expectations and maintain a façade, neglecting their own well-being and inner fulfillment. The more leaders distance themselves from their authentic selves, the more they sacrifice their own happiness and sense of purpose.

Cultivating Authenticity in Enlightened Heart Leadership

Enlightened heart leaders recognize the importance of authenticity and strive to lead from their true selves. They understand that embracing their authentic selves allows for genuine connections, open communication, and a nurturing leadership style. Here are some key strategies for cultivating authenticity in enlightened heart leadership:

- Self-Reflection and Awareness: Enlightened leaders engage in regular self-reflection to explore their values, beliefs, strengths, and weaknesses. They cultivate self-awareness, understanding their authentic desires and motivations. This self-awareness serves as a foundation for authentic leadership. By taking the time to understand their true selves, leaders can align their actions and decisions with their core values and purpose.

- Embracing Vulnerability: Authenticity requires leaders to embrace vulnerability and show up as their true selves, flaws and all. Enlightened leaders create a safe and supportive environment where vulnerability is celebrated and seen as a strength. They recognize that vulnerability fosters trust and connection, allowing individuals to bring their whole selves to work. By embracing vulnerability, leaders encourage their teams to do the same, creating a culture of authenticity and psychological safety.

- Authentic Communication: Enlightened leaders foster open and honest communication, encouraging dialogue that is grounded in authenticity. They listen actively, empathize with others' perspectives, and communicate transparently. Authentic communication builds trust, fosters collaboration, and strengthens relationships. By speaking their truth with empathy and respect, leaders create an environment where diverse opinions are valued, and meaningful conversations thrive.

- Leading with Purpose: Enlightened heart leaders align their leadership with a sense of purpose. They lead from their authentic values and vision, inspiring and motivating others with their genuine commitment to a greater purpose. By leading with purpose, they create a sense of meaning and engagement among their teams. They foster a shared sense of purpose that aligns with the organization's mission, igniting passion and commitment within individuals.

- Self-Care and Well-Being: Enlightened leaders recognize the importance of self-care and well-being in maintaining authenticity. They prioritize self-care practices that nourish their physical, mental, and emotional well-being. By taking care of themselves, they model the importance of holistic well-being for their teams. They create a culture that supports self-care, work-life balance, and overall well-being, allowing individuals to show up authentically and thrive.

- Nurturing Authenticity in the Organizational Culture: Enlightened heart leaders understand that cultivating authenticity goes beyond individual efforts—it also requires creating an organizational culture that supports authenticity. They foster an inclusive and psychologically safe environment where individuals feel encouraged to bring their whole selves to work. They promote diversity, equity, and inclusion, recognizing that diverse perspectives contribute to authentic and innovative solutions. They create opportunities for individuals to develop their authentic selves through personal growth initiatives, coaching, and mentorship. They also encourage self-reflection, personal development, and continuous learning, creating opportunities for individuals to explore their authentic selves and grow.

The pseudo self can present a significant challenge to leaders seeking to practice enlightened heart leadership. However, by understanding the concept of the pseudo self and its impact, leaders can cultivate authenticity and lead from their true selves. Enlightened heart leaders prioritize self-reflection, embrace vulnerability, communicate authentically, lead with purpose, and prioritize self-care. They also foster an organizational culture that supports authenticity and provides a safe space for individuals to bring their authentic selves to work. By embracing authenticity, enlightened heart leaders create meaningful connections, foster trust, and inspire their teams to reach their full potential. May this chapter serve as a guide for leaders seeking to navigate the complexities of the pseudo self and lead with authenticity in their enlightened heart leadership journey.

When we think about the pseudo self, it becomes clear that the greatest lies we tell someone are the lies we tell ourselves. When we try to make an excuse such as "I am too busy today to go out for dinner" to a friend, it is your pseudo self telling us that we are not connected with them anymore. Instead of being radically honest about your friendship, you make up excuses and let the relationship take its course. It is important to listen to your pseudo self and create friendships that are meaningful and align with your own self.

ACCEPTANCE AND BELONGING

Acceptance and belonging are vital aspects of enlightened heart leadership as they foster a supportive and inclusive environment where individuals can thrive and contribute their best. When individuals feel accepted and a sense of belonging, they experience psychological safety. This psychological safety is the belief that one can take risks, express their ideas, and be their authentic selves without fear of judgment or negative consequences. In an environment of psychological safety, individuals are more likely to speak up, share their perspectives, and engage in collaborative problem-solving, leading to increased creativity, innovation, and productivity within the organization. Enlightened heart leaders value empathy and understanding, recognizing that every individual brings unique experiences, strengths, and perspectives. By cultivating an atmosphere of acceptance and belonging, leaders foster empathy and understanding among team members. This enables individuals to connect on a deeper level, appreciate diverse viewpoints, and build strong relationships. When people feel understood and accepted, they are more likely to collaborate effectively and resolve conflicts constructively.

Acceptance and belonging create a space where individuals can be their authentic selves, without the need to conform or hide their true identities. This encourages personal growth, self-expression, and overall well-being. When people are accepted for who they are, they experience a sense of value and self-worth, which positively impacts their motivation, engagement, and job satisfaction. Enlightened heart leaders prioritize the well-being of their team members, understanding that their success is closely tied to the happiness and fulfillment of individuals within the organization. Acceptance and belonging are foundational elements of fostering diversity and inclusion within the organization. Enlightened heart leaders understand the importance of diverse perspectives and experiences in driving innovation and problem-solving. By creating an inclusive environment where all individuals feel valued and respected, leaders cultivate a diverse workforce that can contribute unique insights and approaches. This leads to enhanced creativity, adaptability, and a competitive advantage in today's globalized world.

Acceptance and belonging promote collaboration and team cohesion. When individuals feel accepted and part of a cohesive team, they are more willing to collaborate, share knowledge, and support one another. This creates a collaborative culture where individuals work together towards common goals, leveraging their diverse strengths and talents. Enlightened heart leaders foster a sense of unity and camaraderie, ensuring that every team member feels included, valued, and connected to the collective purpose of the organization. Furthermore, acceptance and belonging contribute to an environment conducive to growth and learning. When individuals feel accepted, they are more open to new ideas, constructive feedback, and personal development opportunities.

In conclusion, acceptance and belonging are crucial in enlightened heart leadership as they create an environment of psychological safety, empathy, authenticity, and well-being. They foster diversity, inclusion, collaboration, and team cohesion while supporting individual growth and learning. By embracing acceptance and belonging, enlightened heart leaders cultivate a culture where individuals can thrive, contribute their unique talents, and collectively achieve the organization's purpose and success.

Self-Acceptance

Self-acceptance of who we are as human beings first leads to belonging. If one doesn't know themselves well or accept themselves for who they are, one will always feel vulnerable and not get a sense of belonging. When one goes outside of self looking for validation, they create a pattern of sabotaging themselves and seeking external opinions. The feeling of safety is an internal phenomenon. As people and leaders, we tend to sabotage ourselves by creating our sense of safety. Leaders need to learn to talk to themselves compassionately. Safety is both external and internal. If our locus of control is external, then we will always allow everything outside of us to govern what is going inside us. On the other hand, if our locus of control is internal, nothing external can impact what is going on inside. When a leader's spiritual disposition, values, and rules of engagement are strong, they would be able to make better decisions and know the impact of their choices precisely.

SUSTAINMENT

Sustainability has become a critical focus in today's world, as leaders across various domains recognize the importance of balancing economic growth with social responsibility and environmental stewardship. In the context of leadership, enlightened heart leaders go beyond the traditional notion of sustainability and embrace a holistic approach that considers the long-term well-being of individuals, organizations, communities, and the planet. This chapter explores how leaders with enlightened hearts approach sustainment, integrating ethical practices, environmental consciousness, and social impact into their leadership philosophy.

Ethical Leadership

Enlightened heart leaders place a strong emphasis on ethical leadership, upholding moral principles and integrity in their decision-making processes. They are guided by a deep sense of responsibility and strive to act in ways that are fair, just, and transparent. By prioritizing ethics, they build trust, credibility, and long-term sustainability within their organizations. They hold themselves accountable to ethical standards and inspire their teams to do the same, creating a culture of integrity and ethical behavior.

Environmental Consciousness

Enlightened heart leaders recognize the interconnectedness between their organizations and the environment. They understand that environmental sustainability is vital for the well-being of future generations and the overall health of the planet. They take proactive measures to minimize their organization's ecological footprint, adopting environmentally friendly practices and promoting sustainability initiatives. Whether through energy conservation, waste reduction, or embracing renewable resources, enlightened leaders prioritize environmental consciousness as a core aspect of sustainment.

Social Impact

Enlightened heart leaders understand the significance of social impact in building sustainable organizations and communities. They actively seek ways to make a positive difference in the lives of their employees, stakeholders, and the broader society. They foster a culture of social responsibility by supporting community initiatives, promoting diversity and inclusion, and addressing social issues through their business practices. By aligning their organization's purpose with social impact, enlightened leaders create a sense of purpose and shared values, attracting individuals who are passionate about making a difference.

Long-Term Vision

Enlightened heart leaders have a long-term vision that extends beyond immediate gains. They consider the future consequences of their actions and make decisions that support sustained success. They prioritize organizational resilience, adapting to changing market conditions, technological advancements, and societal shifts. By fostering a culture of adaptability and continuous learning, enlightened leaders ensure that their organizations remain relevant and thrive in the face of challenges.

Stakeholder Engagement

Enlightened heart leaders recognize the importance of stakeholder engagement in sustainment. They actively involve stakeholders, including employees, customers, suppliers, and communities, in decision-making processes. They seek diverse perspectives and value input from all stakeholders, ensuring that their actions consider the interests of all involved. By engaging stakeholders, enlightened leaders build strong relationships, foster trust, and create a sense of collective ownership and commitment to sustainment efforts.

Measurement and Reporting

Enlightened heart leaders understand the significance of measuring and reporting sustainment efforts. They establish clear metrics and goals to assess their organization's performance in environmental, social, and ethical domains. They regularly communicate progress and challenges to stakeholders, demonstrating transparency and accountability. By measuring and reporting on sustainment initiatives, enlightened leaders not only track progress but also inspire continuous improvement and motivate others to take action.

Sustainment is a fundamental aspect of enlightened heart leadership. By integrating ethical practices, environmental consciousness, and social impact into their leadership philosophy, enlightened leaders create sustainable organizations that thrive in the long run. They prioritize ethical leadership, environmental sustainability, social impact, long-term vision, stakeholder engagement, and measurement and reporting. Through their commitment to sustainment, they not only drive organizational success but also contribute to the well-being of individuals, communities, and the planet. May this chapter serve as a guide for leaders seeking to embrace sustainment as a core pillar of their enlightened heart leadership approach.

TRANQUILITY

In the fast-paced and demanding world of leadership, finding moments of tranquility becomes essential for leaders to maintain balance, clarity, and well-being. Tranquility, a state of calmness and inner peace, plays a vital role in enlightened heart leadership. This essay explores the relationship between tranquility and enlightened heart leadership, highlighting how cultivating tranquility enhances self-awareness, emotional intelligence, decision-making, and the ability to lead with compassion and wisdom.

Cultivating Inner Stillness

Tranquility begins with cultivating inner stillness. Enlightened heart leaders understand the importance of creating space for reflection, contemplation, and self-care. By dedicating time to practices such as meditation, mindfulness, and deep breathing, leaders develop the ability to quiet their minds and connect with their inner selves. This inner stillness serves as a foundation for cultivating tranquility and enables leaders to navigate challenges with greater clarity and presence.

Self-Awareness and Emotional Regulation

Tranquility enhances self-awareness and emotional regulation, which are key elements of enlightened heart leadership. When leaders are tranquil, they become attuned to their emotions, thoughts, and reactions. They develop the ability to observe their own mental and emotional states without judgment or reactivity. This heightened self-awareness allows leaders to manage their emotions effectively, make conscious choices, and respond to situations with equanimity and compassion. By cultivating tranquility, leaders become less driven by external circumstances and more guided by their inner wisdom.

Decision-Making and Clarity

Tranquility brings clarity to decision-making processes. When leaders are in a state of tranquility, their minds are calm and focused, enabling them to see beyond immediate pressures and make decisions from a place of wisdom and clarity. Tranquility allows leaders to step back, assess situations with a broader perspective, and consider the long-term implications of their choices. By making decisions from a tranquil state, leaders can avoid impulsive or reactive responses and instead choose actions that align with their values and the greater good.

Compassionate Leadership

Tranquility supports compassionate leadership. When leaders are tranquil, they are more in touch with their own humanity and the humanity of others. They cultivate empathy and deep listening skills, allowing them to connect with the experiences and emotions of their team members. Tranquility enables leaders to lead with compassion, kindness, and understanding, creating a supportive and inclusive environment. Leaders who embody tranquility inspire trust, foster collaboration, and empower others to grow and thrive.

Resilience and Stress Management

Tranquility contributes to resilience and effective stress management. Leaders with tranquil minds are better equipped to handle stress and adversity. They develop the ability to stay centered, composed, and balanced in the face of challenges. Tranquility enables leaders to maintain perspective, regulate stress responses, and make conscious choices rather than reacting impulsively. By cultivating tranquility, leaders enhance their resilience, navigate difficult situations with grace, and inspire their teams to do the same.

Role Modeling and Well-Being

Tranquility allows leaders to be role models for their teams. When leaders prioritize tranquility and demonstrate its benefits in their own lives, they inspire others to embrace practices that cultivate inner peace and well-being. Leaders who embody tranquility create a positive ripple effect, fostering a culture where well-being is valued and prioritized. By modeling tranquility, leaders encourage their teams to find their own moments of calm amidst the challenges of work and life, leading to increased productivity, engagement, and overall well-being.

Tranquility is an essential component of enlightened heart leadership. By cultivating inner stillness, enhancing self-awareness and emotional regulation, making decisions with clarity, leading with compassion, and prioritizing well-being, leaders create a space for tranquility to flourish. Through their own tranquility, leaders inspire and empower their teams to embrace moments of calm and lead with wisdom and compassion. In the midst of a hectic and demanding world, enlightened heart leaders recognize the transformative power of tranquility in enhancing their leadership effectiveness and creating positive organizational cultures. Our mind is always at war until it just finds whatever its truth is. The art is in surrendering. One cannot force someone to connect with them or manipulate someone to be present with them, but you can show up as connectable. A person can do that with some presence and by surrendering to what's happening in the moment. As per the definition, tranquility is the state of being calm. Being in the flow, to some, is being in their most tranquil state. It ties directly to tranquility. When you're in the flow, you are in awe of the tree, whether it's the forest, the trees, the ocean, or something that always reminds you of the world's vastness.

The attribute and skill a leader needs is the ability to be adaptable because you can only go with the flow if you're adaptable. Adaptability is not being stuck to one's own process, structure, or ego. Many organizations, instead of being adaptable, are establishing standard operating procedures. One can't expect the process structure and systems to fix their people's issues.

It is essential to gain a state of self-tranquility to be able to lead with calmness, using cognitive and logical abilities. Leaders need to develop a practice of checking in with themselves.

One can create their own algorithm of what their tranquil state is. The algorithm may be a blend of your personal preferences to get to a state of calm, such as journaling or meditation, a support network to connect with, and your service to give back. One can attain a sense of tranquility if one anchors themselves into something bigger than themselves.

SELF-ESTEEM AND SELF-WORTH

Self-esteem and self-worth are fundamental aspects of enlightened heart leadership, shaping how leaders perceive themselves, interact with others, and guide their organizations. This essay explores the relationship between self-esteem, self-worth, and enlightened heart leadership, emphasizing how cultivating a healthy sense of self-worth enhances authenticity, resilience, empathy, and the ability to lead with compassion and effectiveness.

Authenticity and Self-Acceptance

Self-esteem and self-worth are closely intertwined with authenticity and self-acceptance. Enlightened heart leaders recognize the importance of embracing their unique qualities and worthiness. By cultivating self-esteem and self-worth, leaders develop an authentic sense of self, free from the need for external validation. This self-acceptance allows leaders to show up as their genuine selves, leading with confidence and inspiring others to do the same.

Resilience and Belief in Self

Self-esteem and self-worth contribute to resilience and belief in oneself, which are crucial for enlightened heart leadership. Leaders with a healthy sense of self-esteem have a strong belief in their abilities and inner worth. They bounce back from setbacks, persevere in the face of challenges, and maintain a positive outlook. Self-esteem fuels the belief that one has the capability to overcome obstacles and achieve success, empowering leaders to navigate difficult situations with determination and optimism.

Empathy and Emotional Intelligence

Self-esteem and self-worth play a vital role in empathy and emotional intelligence for enlightened heart leaders. When leaders have a healthy sense of self-worth, they are better equipped to understand and connect with the experiences and emotions of others. Self-esteem enables leaders to approach interactions with empathy, compassion, and genuine care for the well-being of their team members. By valuing and respecting themselves, leaders can extend the same empathy and respect to others, fostering a culture of support, trust, and collaboration.

Confidence and Effective Decision-Making

Self-esteem and self-worth contribute to confidence and effective decision-making in enlightened heart leadership. Leaders with a positive self-image have confidence in their abilities and judgment. Self-esteem empowers leaders to make sound decisions, take calculated risks, and stand firm in their convictions. Confident leaders inspire trust and motivate others to follow their lead, creating an environment of empowerment and innovation.

Overcoming Limiting Beliefs and Imposter Syndrome

Self-esteem and self-worth help leaders overcome limiting beliefs and imposter syndrome. Enlightened heart leaders recognize their inherent worth and capabilities, challenging self-doubt and negative self-perception. By cultivating self-esteem and self-worth, leaders can transcend the fear of inadequacy and embrace their unique contributions. This allows them to lead with confidence, authenticity, and conviction, inspiring others to do the same.

Supporting and Nurturing Team Members

Self-esteem and self-worth enable leaders to support and nurture the self-esteem of their team members. Enlightened heart leaders understand that fostering a positive and nurturing environment requires empowering individuals and helping them develop a healthy sense of self-worth. By recognizing and appreciating the unique talents and contributions of their team members, leaders cultivate an inclusive culture where everyone feels valued and encouraged to reach their full potential.

Self-esteem and self-worth are foundational elements of enlightened heart leadership. By cultivating a healthy sense of self-worth and self-esteem, leaders enhance authenticity, resilience, empathy, confidence, and effective decision-making. Self-esteem empowers leaders to lead from a place of self-acceptance, embracing their worthiness and inspiring others to do the same. In nurturing their own self-esteem and that of their team members, enlightened heart leaders create a supportive and empowering environment where individuals can thrive and contribute their best.

If one's self-esteem and self-worthiness are low, one might not believe their gut and think others know better. Our life comes down to a six-letter word: choice. There is always a choice that we can make where we choose our tranquility and serenity over anything else. It is an act of self-governance where one can self-regulate and create boundaries to protect themselves from anything harmful. One needs to look at how one supports oneself in different life facets to develop a self-identity as an individual and as a part of a community.

Because leaders are facing increasing uncertainty, chaos, stress, and ambiguity, it is essential that leaders first learn to lead themselves before they can effectively lead others. To that end, push yourself to cultivate and then master the very skills you expect to see in your organizations. It starts with you.

When we don't understand ourselves, we are more likely to succumb to the fundamental attribution error of believing that the behaviors of others are the result of negative intent or character ("he was late because he does not want to be in the meeting") and believing that our own behaviors are caused by circumstance ("I was late because of traffic").

Anyone with low internal self-esteem, worthiness, and/or awareness typically see their beliefs and values as "the truth," as opposed to what is true for them based on their feelings and past experiences. We can fail to recognize that others may have equally valid perspectives. As leaders, we need cultivate a daily practice where we check in with ourselves in different facets to develop a self-identity as an individual and as a part of a community.

In the following chapters, we will explore other key principles of enlightened heart leadership and how they can be applied in various leadership contexts.

CHAPTER SEVEN

Creating a Vision for the Future

"As the biggest library if it is in disorder is not as useful as a small but well-arranged one, so you may accumulate a vast amount of knowledge but it will be of far less value than a much smaller amount if you have not thought it over for yourself."
— Arthur Schopenhauer

Creating a vision for the business is a transformative process that requires the guiding hand of an enlightened heart leader. Such leaders embark on this journey by first engaging in self-reflection and aligning their own values and purpose with those of the organization. By understanding their own authentic aspirations, they can craft a vision that resonates deeply with their core being. This alignment serves as the foundation for a vision that is not only compelling but also authentic and inspiring.

An enlightened heart leader recognizes the importance of mindful listening and empathy

Illustration: Shutterstock

in the visioning process. They actively listen to the needs, desires, and aspirations of their team members, customers, and stakeholders. By cultivating empathy, they gain a deep understanding of the diverse perspectives and challenges that exist within the organization and its ecosystem. This empathetic understanding allows them to craft a vision that addresses the collective needs and aspirations of all stakeholders, fostering a sense of inclusivity and shared purpose. Involving stakeholders at all levels of the organization is a key aspect of an enlightened heart leader's approach to vision creation. They create an environment of open dialogue and collaboration, where diverse voices are encouraged and valued. By engaging individuals from various backgrounds and roles, the leader taps into the collective wisdom and expertise of the entire team. This collaborative process not only enriches the vision but also creates a sense of ownership and commitment among team members.

Clarity and inspiration are vital in articulating the vision to the organization. An enlightened heart leader communicates the vision with simplicity, ensuring that it is easily understood and remembered by all. They paint a vivid picture of the future, highlighting the positive impact the organization can make. By conveying the vision in an inspiring manner, the leader captures the hearts and minds of individuals, motivating them to actively contribute to its realization. An enlightened heart leader recognizes the importance of aligning the vision with the purpose of the organization. They help individuals understand how their work contributes to a greater good and creates meaning in their lives. By establishing this connection, the leader instills a sense of purpose and fulfillment in the entire organization, fostering a culture of engagement and commitment.

The journey towards realizing the vision is not a linear path. An enlightened heart leader embraces continuous learning and adaptation. They foster a culture of innovation and agility, encouraging individuals to challenge assumptions, embrace change, and refine the vision as the organization grows and evolves. By maintaining a learning mindset and promoting a culture of curiosity, the leader ensures that the vision remains relevant and adaptable to the ever-changing business landscape.

Sustainability and ethical practices are integral to an enlightened heart leader's vision. They consider the long-term impact of the business on the environment, society, and all stakeholders. The vision reflects a commitment to responsible business practices, social responsibility, and ethical decision-making. By embedding sustainability and ethics into the vision, the leader ensures that the organization not only thrives financially but also contributes positively to the well-being of all stakeholders and the wider community.

Lastly, an enlightened heart leader understands the importance of creating an emotional connection and providing support throughout the visioning process. They address the deeper aspirations and values of individuals, making them feel valued and heard. By fostering a sense of belonging, trust, and commitment, the leader ensures that individuals are emotionally invested in the vision and motivated to work towards its realization. Through guidance, encouragement, and support, the leader empowers individuals to align their personal goals with the vision, creating a unified and purpose-driven organization. Creating a vision for the business requires the wisdom, compassion, and authenticity of an enlightened heart leader. By aligning personal values, practicing mindful listening, engaging stakeholders, inspiring with clarity, connecting with purpose, embracing learning and adaptation, promoting sustainability and ethics, and nurturing emotional connection, an enlightened heart leader crafts a vision that guides the organization towards a future of shared purpose, growth, and positive impact.

In order to be effective leaders, individuals must be able to envision a better future for their organizations. In this chapter, we will explore the importance of creating a vision for the future and how it can help leaders to inspire their team members. We will discuss the principles of goal-setting and how leaders can create a shared sense of purpose within their organizations.

As a leader, creating a vision for your team or organization is one of the most important tasks you will undertake. A clear and compelling vision can inspire your team members, align their efforts, and drive your organization towards its goals. However, creating a vision is not simply a matter of coming up with a set of goals or objectives. It requires a deep understanding of your organization's purpose, values, and unique strengths.

Creating a vision with an enlightened heart approach begins with understanding your organization's purpose. The purpose is the reason why your organization exists, and it should guide everything you do. It's important to take the time to reflect on your purpose and ask yourself questions such as:

- What problems do we solve for our customers or clients?
- What unique strengths do we bring to the table?
- What values do we hold dear?

By understanding your purpose, you can create a vision that reflects your organization's unique strengths and values. Creating a vision with an enlightened heart approach requires a deep understanding of your organization's purpose, values, and unique strengths. By cultivating qualities such as empathy, compassion, and self-awareness, leaders can create a vision that inspires and motivates their team members. A compelling vision can align your team members' efforts, drive your organization towards its goals, and create a sense of purpose and meaning for everyone involved.

Creating a vision with an enlightened heart approach also requires cultivating qualities such as empathy, compassion, and self-awareness. When leaders approach vision-setting with an enlightened heart, they can:

- Listen Deeply: By listening carefully to team members' perspectives and concerns, leaders can gain a deeper understanding of their organization's strengths and weaknesses.

- Practice Empathy: Leaders who understand their team members' perspectives and challenges are better able to create a vision that resonates with their team.

- Be Self-Aware: Leaders who are aware of their own biases and emotions can create a vision that is more inclusive and reflective of their organization's values.

Once you have a clear understanding of your organization's purpose and have cultivated an enlightened heart, you can begin to create a vision that inspires and motivates your team members. A compelling vision should:

- Be Clear and Concise: A vision that is too complex or vague can be difficult for team members to understand and rally behind.

- Be Aligned with Your Purpose: Your vision should reflect your organization's purpose and values.

- Be Aspirational: Your vision should challenge your team members to aspire to something greater than the status quo.

- Be Inclusive: Your vision should be inclusive and reflect the diverse perspectives and experiences of your team members.

- Be Communicated Effectively: Your vision should be communicated clearly and consistently to your team members.

CURIOSITY AND CREATION

Curiosity is a powerful catalyst for growth, learning, and innovation. It fuels the flames of exploration, propelling individuals and organizations to new frontiers of knowledge and understanding. In the context of enlightened heart leadership, curiosity takes on a special significance. It becomes not just a tool for personal and professional development but a key attribute that fosters a deeper connection with oneself, others, and the world at large.

Enlightened heart leadership goes beyond conventional notions of leadership. It is a transformative approach that integrates wisdom, compassion, and mindfulness into the leadership journey. At its core, it recognizes the interconnectedness of all beings and the importance of leading from a place of authenticity and purpose. In this context, curiosity becomes a guiding force that drives leaders to explore the depths of their own being, the dynamics of human relationships, and the broader context in which their organizations operate.

Curiosity is the spark that ignites the flame of self-discovery. It prompts enlightened heart leaders to embark on a profound inner journey of introspection and self-awareness. They embrace a curious mindset that compels them to question their beliefs, assumptions, and biases. Through this process, they gain insights into their true essence, values, and purpose, allowing them to lead with greater clarity, integrity, and authenticity. In the realm of enlightened heart leadership, curiosity extends beyond the individual leader. It permeates the organizational culture and becomes the driving force behind a collective thirst for knowledge and growth. Curious leaders recognize the immense value in fostering a culture of curiosity within their organizations. They encourage their teams to ask questions, challenge the status quo, and explore new possibilities. This culture of curiosity cultivates an environment of intellectual curiosity, creativity, and innovation, where ideas can flourish and solutions can be discovered.

Curiosity also enhances the empathetic nature of enlightened heart leaders. It drives them to seek a deeper understanding of the experiences, perspectives, and needs of others. Curious leaders listen with genuine interest and suspend judgment, creating space for meaningful connections and compassionate leadership. By engaging in curious inquiry, they bridge gaps of understanding, build trust, and foster a sense of belonging and psychological safety within their teams. Furthermore, curiosity enables enlightened heart leaders to embrace change and navigate uncertainty with resilience and adaptability. They approach change with a curious mindset, viewing it as an opportunity for growth and transformation. Curiosity empowers leaders to explore new strategies, experiment with different approaches, and learn from both successes and failures. It fuels the courage to step into the unknown and embrace the challenges that come with leading in a rapidly changing world.

In this essay, we delve into the profound relationship between curiosity and enlightened heart leadership. We explore how curiosity deepens self-awareness, fosters empathetic connections, drives innovation, and enhances adaptability. We examine how enlightened heart leaders cultivate curiosity within themselves and their organizations, creating an environment that nurtures growth, learning, and positive change. By harnessing the power of curiosity, enlightened heart leaders unlock their own potential and inspire others to embark on a lifelong journey of discovery and transformation.

The Power of Curiosity

Curiosity is the innate human drive to seek knowledge, explore new ideas, and question the status quo. Enlightened heart leaders recognize that curiosity opens the door to new possibilities and fresh perspectives. They harness the power of curiosity to transcend limitations, challenge assumptions, and discover innovative solutions to complex problems. Curiosity fuels a continuous quest for improvement, propelling leaders to constantly seek knowledge, expand their horizons, and push the boundaries of what is possible.

Curiosity and Self-Awareness

Curiosity is a pathway to self-awareness, which is a cornerstone of enlightened heart leadership. Curious leaders embark on an inward journey of exploration, seeking to understand their own strengths, weaknesses, values, and motivations. By cultivating a curious mindset, leaders gain insights into their own patterns of thinking, biases, and blind spots. This self-awareness allows them to lead with authenticity, humility, and a willingness to learn from others. Curiosity fuels the introspection needed to continuously evolve as leaders and connect with their own true purpose.

Fostering a Culture of Curiosity

Enlightened heart leaders understand the importance of fostering a culture of curiosity within their organizations. They create an environment that encourages questioning, experimentation, and intellectual curiosity. Leaders promote a safe space for individuals to express their ideas, challenge existing norms, and explore new possibilities. By valuing curiosity, they stimulate a sense of intellectual adventure, curiosity-driven learning, and a thirst for knowledge throughout the organization. This culture of curiosity nurtures innovation, creativity, and a growth mindset among team members.

Curiosity and Empathy

Curiosity enhances empathy, an essential quality for enlightened heart leaders. Curious leaders actively seek to understand the perspectives, experiences, and needs of others. They ask thoughtful questions, listen deeply, and suspend judgment, creating a space for genuine connection and empathy. Curiosity enables leaders to step into the shoes of others, fostering a sense of compassion, inclusivity, and understanding. By embracing curiosity, leaders build bridges of empathy, strengthening relationships and trust within their teams and with stakeholders.

Embracing Change and Adaptability

Curiosity fuels a mindset of embracing change and adaptability in enlightened heart leadership. Curious leaders are open to new ideas, emerging trends, and different approaches. They actively seek out opportunities to learn and grow, even in the face of uncertainty and ambiguity. By approaching change with curiosity, leaders become agile and adaptable, leading their organizations through transformation and navigating complex challenges with resilience and grace. Curiosity allows leaders to see change as an opportunity for growth rather than a threat, inspiring others to embrace change as well.

Curiosity and Lifelong Learning

Enlightened heart leaders embody a lifelong learning mindset, and curiosity is the driving force behind it. Curiosity fuels a thirst for knowledge, a hunger to explore new disciplines, and a desire to continually expand one's intellectual horizons. Leaders actively seek out diverse sources of information, engage in self-directed learning, and encourage a culture of continuous learning within their organizations. Curiosity propels leaders to stay ahead of industry trends, seek out innovative solutions, and inspire a culture of intellectual curiosity among their team members.

Curiosity is a fundamental attribute of enlightened heart leadership, empowering leaders to embrace change, cultivate self-awareness, foster empathy, and inspire a culture of innovation and continuous learning. By harnessing the power of curiosity, leaders unlock their own potential and ignite the curiosity of others, leading to transformative outcomes for themselves and their organizations. In the realm of enlightened heart leadership, curiosity serves as a guiding light, illuminating new paths, expanding horizons, and paving the way for growth and success.

Our environment impacts how we think, feel, and do and shapes us as a person because of our experiences. When you live your life with curiosity, you experience a much wider spectrum of colors, a broader experience of the world, to form your own decisions. Being curious allows us to look at all the different ways people label their own values and beliefs, as it helps us create our own beliefs or thoughts. As a leader, one is more effective if they are curious and have a worldly view of things.

PURPOSE AND CREATION

The purpose of one's life and existence is bigger than oneself. If one is not connected to their purpose, one will not feel anchored or attached to anything. When one is anchored to their purpose, then their dedication and likelihood to commit to something become higher.

Enlightened heart leaders understand that a sense of purpose is not merely a superficial concept or a catchy mission statement. It is a profound force that drives individuals and organizations towards meaningful and impactful outcomes. Purpose serves as a compass, guiding actions, decisions, and priorities. It taps into the deeper yearnings and aspirations of individuals, aligning them with a higher calling that goes beyond personal gain or material success. In the realm of enlightened heart leadership, purpose takes on a transformative significance. It becomes the foundation upon which leaders build their vision, values, and actions. Purpose becomes the driving force that fuels motivation, resilience, and commitment, not only for the leader but also for the entire organization. When individuals connect with a sense of purpose, they become intrinsically motivated, driven by a deep sense of meaning and fulfillment in their work.

Enlightened heart leaders embark on a journey of self-discovery to uncover their own authentic purpose. They engage in introspection, reflecting on their values, passions, and the impact they want to make in the world. They understand that their personal purpose serves as the anchor from which they lead, inspiring and guiding others towards a shared vision. By understanding their own purpose, they create a powerful foundation that allows them to lead with authenticity, passion, and a deep sense of integrity. Moreover, enlightened heart leaders recognize the importance of aligning personal purpose with the purpose of the organization. They understand that when individuals' personal purposes harmonize with the overarching purpose of the organization, a sense of shared purpose emerges. This alignment creates a powerful synergy, where individuals are not just working towards their own goals but are united in a collective mission. It fosters a sense of belonging, connection, and a shared commitment to a higher cause. To instill a sense of purpose within the organization, enlightened heart leaders effectively communicate a compelling vision that inspires and resonates with others. They paint a vivid picture of the future, articulating the positive impact the organization can have on individuals, communities, or society as a whole. This vision serves as a North Star, guiding individuals' efforts and igniting their passion and commitment.

Through effective communication, leaders engage hearts and minds, cultivating a sense of purpose that transcends the mundane and propels individuals towards extraordinary achievements. Enlightened heart leaders empower individuals by providing autonomy and opportunities for mastery. They create an environment where individuals have the freedom to make decisions, pursue their passions, and take ownership of their work. By nurturing a culture of growth and development, leaders enable individuals to master their skills, make meaningful contributions aligned with their purpose, and experience a sense of achievement and fulfillment. This empowerment reinforces the sense of purpose and fosters a strong sense of engagement and commitment. In addition, enlightened heart leaders emphasize the importance of connection and impact. They foster a culture of collaboration, where individuals understand how their contributions fit into the larger picture. By highlighting the significance of each person's role and the positive impact they have on others, leaders reinforce the sense of purpose. They celebrate achievements, acknowledge the value of individual efforts, and create a supportive community that strengthens the collective purpose.

Creating a sense of purpose is a transformative process in enlightened heart leadership. It is not a one-time endeavor but an ongoing journey of self-discovery, alignment, and communication. When individuals connect with their purpose and align it with the broader organizational purpose, a powerful sense of shared purpose emerges. This sense of purpose fuels motivation, engagement, and commitment, leading to a harmonious and thriving organizational culture. Through purpose-driven leadership, enlightened heart leaders inspire individuals to reach their full potential, contribute meaningfully to the organization's mission, and make a positive impact on the world.

Understanding the Essence of Purpose

Purpose goes beyond the pursuit of profit or accomplishing tasks. It is a higher calling that aligns with the values, passions, and aspirations of individuals and organizations. Enlightened heart leaders delve into introspection and self-reflection to uncover their own authentic purpose. They reflect on their values, personal experiences, and the impact they want to make in the world. By understanding their own purpose, they create a foundation from which they can inspire and guide others.

Aligning Personal and Organizational Purpose

Enlightened heart leaders recognize the importance of aligning personal purpose with the purpose of the organization. They engage in deep conversations with team members to understand their individual aspirations, strengths, and values. By fostering a culture of open dialogue, they create an environment where personal purpose can be woven into the fabric of the organizational purpose. Through this alignment, leaders create a sense of shared purpose, tapping into the collective potential of the team.

Communicating a Compelling Vision

To instill a sense of purpose, enlightened heart leaders articulate a compelling vision that inspires and resonates with others. They craft a clear and vivid picture of the future, highlighting the positive impact the organization can have on individuals, communities, or society as a whole. By painting this vision, leaders create a sense of purpose that transcends individual tasks and connects people to a larger, meaningful mission. Through effective communication, they engage hearts and minds, fueling a sense of purpose and rallying others to work towards a common goal.

Empowering Autonomy and Mastery

Enlightened heart leaders understand that a sense of purpose flourishes when individuals have autonomy and the opportunity for mastery. They foster an environment where team members have the freedom to make decisions, pursue their passions, and take ownership of their work. By providing opportunities for growth and development, leaders empower individuals to master their skills and make meaningful contributions aligned with their purpose. This autonomy and mastery reinforce the sense of purpose, leading to increased engagement and a sense of fulfillment.

Fostering Connection and Impact

Enlightened heart leaders create a sense of purpose by fostering connection and emphasizing the impact of individuals' work. They cultivate a culture of collaboration, where individuals understand how their contributions fit into the larger picture. By highlighting the significance of each person's role and the positive impact they have on others, leaders reinforce the sense of purpose. They celebrate achievements, acknowledge the value of individual efforts, and create a supportive community that strengthens the collective purpose.

Embodying Servant Leadership

Enlightened heart leaders embody the principles of servant leadership, recognizing that their role is to serve others and the greater good. They prioritize the growth, well-being, and development of their team members. By nurturing a culture of care and compassion, leaders create an environment where individuals feel valued, supported, and inspired to live their purpose. Through their actions and behaviors, they model the values and principles that underpin the organization's purpose, creating a ripple effect of purpose-driven actions throughout the organization.

Embracing Adaptability and Learning

Enlightened heart leaders understand that purpose is not a static concept but evolves with changing circumstances. They encourage adaptability and a growth mindset, embracing new challenges as opportunities for learning and expansion. By promoting a culture of continuous learning, leaders inspire individuals to explore new possibilities, embrace change, and adapt their purpose in alignment with the evolving needs of the organization and the world.

In the realm of enlightened heart leadership, creating a sense of purpose is a transformative process that ignites passion, engagement, and fulfillment. By understanding and aligning personal and organizational purpose, communicating a compelling vision, empowering autonomy and mastery, fostering connection and impact, embodying servant leadership, and embracing adaptability and learning, enlightened heart leaders inspire individuals to connect with their purpose and contribute to a higher collective mission. Through purpose-driven leadership, organizations thrive, and individuals find meaning and joy in their work, creating a positive ripple effect that extends beyond the boundaries of the organization.

SOUL SIGNATURE

Enlightened heart leadership goes beyond traditional leadership paradigms by recognizing the profound spiritual dimension that underlies human existence. At its core lies the concept of the soul signature, a unique and authentic expression of our innermost essence.

In this essay, we delve into the meaning and significance of the soul signature in the context of enlightened heart leadership, exploring how it shapes and informs the way leaders navigate their roles, inspire others, and create transformative change. The soul signature represents the essence of who we truly are at the deepest level of our being. It goes beyond societal labels, roles, and external achievements, delving into the core aspects of our identity. It encompasses our innate gifts, passions, values, and purpose. It is the radiant energy that emanates from within, reflecting the authenticity of our souls. The soul signature is an invitation to embrace our true selves, transcending the limitations of ego and societal expectations.

Enlightened heart leaders embark on a profound journey of self-discovery to uncover their soul signature. They recognize that their leadership effectiveness and impact are deeply rooted in their ability to connect with their authentic selves. By understanding their soul signature, leaders gain profound insights into their purpose, values, and unique contributions to the world. They cultivate a deep sense of self-awareness that serves as a compass, guiding their decisions, actions, and interactions with others.

Moreover, the relationship between the soul signature and enlightened heart leadership goes beyond the individual level. It extends to the collective consciousness of the organization or team. When leaders are connected with their soul signature, they create a ripple effect that resonates with others. Their authenticity and alignment inspire those around them to connect with their own soul signatures, fostering a culture of individual empowerment and collective growth. This shared sense of purpose and authenticity nurtures a deep sense of belonging, psychological safety, and a shared commitment to a higher collective vision.

The practice of enlightened heart leadership requires leaders to engage in self-reflection, introspection, and self-care to cultivate a deep connection with their soul signature. They create dedicated time and space for inner exploration, embracing practices such as meditation, journaling, and contemplation. Through these practices, leaders gain clarity, deepen their self-awareness, and cultivate a state of presence that allows them to lead from a place of authenticity and wisdom.

Additionally, enlightened heart leaders recognize that the soul signature is not a static concept but a dynamic and evolving expression of our essence. They understand that the journey of soulful leadership requires continuous growth and learning. Leaders seek wisdom from various sources, such as spiritual teachings, mentors, and diverse perspectives, to expand their understanding of their soul signature and its interconnectedness with the world. This ongoing exploration allows leaders to integrate spiritual principles and values into their leadership approach, infusing their actions with compassion, empathy, and a reverence for the inherent worth of all beings.

The soul signature holds a significant role in enlightened heart leadership. It represents the unique and authentic expression of our inner essence, guiding leaders to lead from a place of deep self-awareness, purpose, and authenticity. As leaders connect with their soul signature, they inspire and empower others to do the same, fostering a culture of individual growth, collective transformation, and meaningful impact. The exploration and cultivation of the soul signature becomes a transformative journey that propels leaders towards enlightened heart leadership, creating a positive ripple effect that extends far beyond the boundaries of their organizations and into the world.

Understanding the Soul Signature

The soul signature represents the unique energetic imprint of an individual's soul. It goes beyond the external labels and roles we assume in the world. It reflects the essence of our being, encompassing our values, passions, strengths, and the purpose that drives us. The soul signature is like a fingerprint, distinct and unparalleled, reflecting the true nature of our soul. It holds the key to our authenticity, guiding us to align our actions and leadership with our deepest truths.

Enlightened heart leaders embark on a journey of self-discovery to understand and embrace their soul signature. They delve into introspection and self-reflection, seeking to uncover their true essence beyond societal expectations and external influences. By connecting with their soul signature, leaders gain clarity and insight into their purpose, values, and authentic self. This profound self-awareness becomes the guiding compass for their leadership journey, shaping their decisions, actions, and relationships.

The Relationship between Soul Signature and Enlightened Heart Leadership

Enlightened heart leadership recognizes that the soul signature holds the key to leading with authenticity, compassion, and wisdom. When leaders are aligned with their soul signature, they access a wellspring of inner guidance and intuition. They tap into a deeper level of understanding and empathy, transcending the limitations of the ego and embracing a more expansive perspective. This alignment allows leaders to make decisions and take actions that are in alignment with their true selves, fostering a profound sense of integrity and purpose.

Moreover, the soul signature provides a source of inspiration and resilience for enlightened heart leaders. When they lead from their authentic selves, they embody a deep sense of passion and purpose that resonates with others. Their words and actions are infused with a genuine and magnetic energy that inspires trust, engagement, and commitment. By living in alignment with their soul signature, leaders become beacons of light, guiding others to connect with their own authentic selves and unlock their unique potential.

The soul signature also plays a crucial role in fostering meaningful connections and relationships within organizations. When leaders are attuned to their own soul signature, they create a space that invites others to show up authentically and fully. By embracing and valuing the diverse soul signatures of team members, enlightened heart leaders cultivate an inclusive and empowering culture. This culture encourages individuals to bring their whole selves to work, fostering a sense of belonging, psychological safety, and collective growth.

The Practice of Soulful Leadership

Enlightened heart leaders actively cultivate their connection with their soul signature through practices that nurture self-reflection, mindfulness, and self-care. They engage in activities such as meditation, journaling, and introspective exercises that deepen their understanding of their own soul signature. By dedicating time and space for inner exploration, leaders enhance their self-awareness, align their actions with their authentic selves, and cultivate a state of presence and openness in their interactions with others.

Furthermore, enlightened heart leaders recognize that soulful leadership is a continuous journey of growth and evolution. They embrace opportunities for learning, personal development, and spiritual exploration. By seeking wisdom from various sources, such as mentors, spiritual teachings, and nature, leaders expand their understanding of their soul signature and its connection to the greater universe. This ongoing exploration allows them to integrate spiritual principles into their leadership approach, infusing their actions with compassion, interconnectedness, and a reverence for the inherent worth of all beings.

The soul signature holds a profound significance in enlightened heart leadership. It represents the unique essence of individuals and provides a compass for leading with authenticity, compassion, and wisdom. As leaders connect with their soul signature, they unlock their true potential, inspiring others to do the same. By embracing their soul signature, leaders foster a culture of authenticity, empower individuals to bring their whole selves to work, and create an environment that cultivates deep connection, purpose, and growth. In the journey of enlightened heart leadership, the soul signature becomes a guiding light, illuminating the path towards transformative leadership and a more enlightened world.

The term "soul signature" in leadership refers to the unique blend of qualities, values, beliefs, and strengths that define an individual leader's style and approach. It is the essence of who they are as a person and how they show up in their leadership role. A leader's soul signature can influence how they interact with their team, how they make decisions, and how they approach challenges. It is the authentic expression of their leadership, reflecting their innermost values and beliefs.

BALANCE AND SUSTAINMENT

In the dynamic landscape of leadership, the concept of balance takes on a profound significance for those embracing the path of enlightened heart leadership. It transcends the traditional notions of work-life balance, extending to a holistic approach that integrates the diverse dimensions of our existence. Enlightened heart leaders recognize that achieving balance is not just about managing competing demands but about harmonizing and nourishing all aspects of life. In this essay, we delve into the multifaceted concept of balance and explore its vital role in enlightened heart leadership, examining how leaders can cultivate equilibrium and thrive in their personal and professional lives.

Understanding Balance

Balance, in the context of enlightened heart leadership, goes beyond a mere equilibrium between work and personal life. It encompasses a more expansive perspective that recognizes the interplay between different domains of life, including work, relationships, self-care, personal growth, and spiritual well-being. It is the art of skillfully navigating the complexities of leadership while maintaining harmony within oneself and with the world around us. Balance is not a fixed state but a dynamic process of continuous adjustment and conscious integration, allowing leaders to adapt to the ever-changing demands of their roles.

The Role of Balance in Enlightened Heart Leadership

Enlightened heart leaders understand that finding and maintaining balance is crucial for their well-being, effectiveness, and sustained impact. They recognize that when they are in a state of balance, they can lead with clarity, wisdom, and compassion. By tending to their own well-being and harmonizing the various dimensions of their lives, they create a solid foundation that supports their leadership journey and empowers them to navigate challenges with resilience and grace. Balance also plays a significant role in fostering authenticity and presence in enlightened heart leadership. When leaders prioritize balance, they cultivate self-awareness, align their actions with their values, and show up authentically in all aspects of their lives. By integrating their personal and professional selves, they bring their whole selves to their roles, leading with integrity and creating meaningful connections with others. This authenticity and presence not only inspire trust and confidence but also set a powerful example for others to follow.

Practicing Balance

Enlightened heart leaders employ various practices and strategies to cultivate balance in their lives. They understand that balance is not a one-size-fits-all concept but a deeply personal and individual journey. They engage in self-reflection to gain clarity on their priorities, values, and aspirations, allowing them to make conscious choices that align with their vision of a balanced life. This self-reflection helps leaders identify areas of imbalance and provides an opportunity for intentional adjustments and realignment.

Mindfulness is another essential practice embraced by enlightened heart leaders to cultivate balance. By cultivating present-moment awareness, they are better able to manage stress, stay focused, and make thoughtful decisions. Mindfulness practices such as meditation, breathing exercises, and mindful movement allow leaders to develop a deep sense of inner calm and resilience, enabling them to navigate challenges and conflicts with greater equanimity.

Furthermore, enlightened heart leaders understand the importance of setting boundaries. They establish clear boundaries between their professional and personal lives, ensuring that they have dedicated time and space for self-care, relaxation, and rejuvenation. By setting boundaries, leaders create a healthy separation between their work responsibilities and personal commitments, preventing burnout and promoting overall well-being.

Balance serves as a cornerstone of enlightened heart leadership, enabling leaders to navigate the complexities of their roles with grace, authenticity, and resilience. By embracing balance, leaders cultivate a sense of harmony and integration in their personal and professional lives, nurturing their well-being and fostering meaningful connections with others. Through self-reflection, mindfulness practices, and the establishment of boundaries, leaders develop the skills and awareness necessary to navigate the demands of leadership while tending to their own needs and maintaining a sense of equilibrium. In doing so, they set an inspiring example and create a positive ripple effect, encouraging others to seek balance and well-being in their own paths of enlightened heart leadership.

VALUES

In the realm of enlightened heart leadership, values play a vital and transformative role in shaping the leader's perspective, actions, and impact. At its core, enlightened heart leadership goes beyond traditional leadership paradigms by emphasizing the integration of compassion, empathy, and authenticity into every aspect of leadership. Values serve as the foundation upon which enlightened heart leaders build their leadership philosophy, guiding their decision-making, shaping their relationships, and driving their vision for a better world.

Enlightened heart leadership stands in contrast to conventional leadership approaches that often prioritize financial success, power dynamics, and self-interest. It recognizes that true leadership extends beyond personal gain and encompasses a deep commitment to the well-being and interconnectedness of all beings. Values in enlightened heart leadership reflect this expanded understanding and guide leaders to act in ways that benefit not just themselves or their organizations, but also the broader community and the world at large.

Values form the essence of enlightened heart leadership, serving as guiding principles that inspire and inform every aspect of a leader's role. These values are deeply rooted in compassion, empathy, authenticity, inclusivity, and sustainability. They go beyond individual preferences or societal norms and reflect a fundamental belief in the inherent worth and interconnectedness of all individuals and the natural world. Enlightened heart leaders understand that values act as a moral compass, providing direction and clarity in decision-making. These values guide leaders to make choices that prioritize the greater good, taking into account the well-being and interests of all stakeholders involved. By aligning their actions with their values, leaders create a foundation of trust, integrity, and accountability within their teams and organizations.

Values in enlightened heart leadership are not merely conceptual ideals or empty rhetoric. They serve as the driving force behind actions and decisions. When leaders embody and live their values, they create a powerful ripple effect that permeates the organizational culture and influences the behavior of others. By consistently aligning their actions with their values, leaders inspire and empower their teams to do the same, fostering a culture of authenticity, respect, and purpose. Values also play a crucial role in shaping the leader's authenticity and congruence. When leaders lead from a place of deep alignment with their values, they demonstrate consistency between their words and deeds. This authenticity creates an environment of psychological safety, where team members feel encouraged to express themselves openly, take risks, and contribute their unique perspectives.

Moreover, values in enlightened heart leadership serve as a catalyst for personal growth and transformation. As leaders continuously reflect upon and refine their values, they deepen their self-awareness and expand their consciousness. This inner journey of aligning values with actions leads to a greater sense of purpose, meaning, and fulfillment in their leadership journey. It also allows leaders to continuously learn and grow, adapting their values to meet the evolving needs of their organization and the world.

Values in enlightened heart leadership differ from conventional leadership approaches in significant ways. While conventional leadership may prioritize financial success, competition, and external recognition, enlightened heart leadership places a higher value on compassion, empathy, respect, and service to others. It recognizes that true leadership extends beyond material gains and focuses on creating a positive and transformative impact on individuals, communities, and the planet. Furthermore, values in enlightened heart leadership are not static or rigid. They evolve and expand as leaders gain new insights and understanding. Enlightened heart leaders engage in ongoing self-reflection, dialogue, and self-inquiry to ensure that their values remain aligned with their evolving understanding and the needs of the changing world. This commitment to continuous growth and alignment with values sets enlightened heart leaders apart, enabling them to navigate complexity with wisdom, compassion, and ethical integrity.

Values lie at the heart of enlightened heart leadership, providing a solid foundation for ethical decision-making, authentic relationships, and visionary leadership. In the pursuit of creating a more compassionate and interconnected world, enlightened heart leaders prioritize values such as compassion, empathy, authenticity, inclusivity, and sustainability. By embodying these values and aligning their actions with their principles, enlightened heart leaders inspire positive change, foster meaningful connections, and create organizations and communities that thrive on a foundation of shared values.

The Essence of Values in Enlightened Heart Leadership

Enlightened heart leadership places a strong emphasis on aligning actions with deeply held values. Unlike traditional leadership approaches that may prioritize short-term gains or external measures of success, enlightened heart leadership recognizes the intrinsic worth and interconnectedness of all beings. It is rooted in a set of values that reflect compassion, empathy, authenticity, inclusivity, and sustainability. Values act as a moral compass that guides leaders in making decisions that honor the greater good, considering the well-being of all stakeholders and the impact on the broader community and environment. These values go beyond personal gain and extend to creating a positive and transformative impact that transcends immediate circumstances.

The Role of Values in Enlightened Heart Leadership

Values provide a framework for ethical decision-making in enlightened heart leadership. They help leaders navigate complex situations, dilemmas, and conflicts with integrity and compassion. By grounding their actions in their values, leaders ensure that their decisions are consistent with their deepest beliefs and principles, fostering trust, accountability, and transparency within their teams and organizations. Moreover, values in enlightened heart leadership shape the leader's authenticity and congruence. When leaders align their actions with their values, they demonstrate consistency between their words and deeds, enhancing trust and credibility. This alignment fosters an environment of psychological safety, where team members feel comfortable expressing themselves and contributing to the collective mission. Values also serve as a catalyst for personal growth and transformation. Enlightened heart leaders continuously examine and refine their values, allowing them to deepen their self-awareness and expand their consciousness. By exploring the alignment between their values and actions, leaders become more attuned to their authentic selves, developing a deeper sense of purpose, meaning, and fulfillment in their leadership journey.

The Distinction of Values in Enlightened Heart Leadership

Values are the bedrock of enlightened heart leadership, providing a moral compass and guiding principles for leaders to navigate their roles with authenticity, integrity, and compassion.

They shape decision-making, influence organizational culture, and inspire meaningful transformation. By prioritizing values such as compassion, empathy, authenticity, and sustainability, enlightened heart leaders create a positive and inclusive environment that fosters personal and collective growth. Values serve as a beacon, leading the way towards a more compassionate and interconnected world where leadership is driven by purpose, ethics, and a deep sense of responsibility.

Values lay the foundation for ethical leadership. It establishes the foundation of the organizational culture. It is essential to have a balanced value scorecard that helps in measuring effectiveness along functional lines and operationalize integrity. Many have written about values and value proposition. At least in theory, every successful company operates according to an effective business model. By systematically identifying all of its constituent parts, leaders can understand how the model fulfills a potential value proposition in a profitable way using certain key resources and key processes. That is the idea. The challenge of course is in recognizing and creating a potential value proposition. A critical attribute of a customer value proposition is its precision: how perfectly it aligns with the customer job to be done. But such precision is often the most difficult thing to achieve. Companies trying to create a new value proposition often attempt to do too much and miss the mark defining the one job they must fulfill. Truly great leaders understand the difference between what should never change and what should be open for change, between what is genuinely sacred and what is not. This rare ability to manage continuity and change—requiring a consciously practiced discipline—is closely linked to the ability to develop a value proposition.

A useful place to start in creating a value proposition with precision is in filling out a Values (Big Bold Steps) Balanced Scorecard. A template has been provided below. It will also be available in the accompanied workbook. Again, the idea here is to operationalize what you stand for. Scan your environment to notice values along these lines and attempt to fill out the scorecard. This will not be a one-and-done exercise. Instead, to be effective, create a practice where checking in with your values, as operationalized in your life, becomes part of your personal and organizational practice.

Values (Big Bold Steps) Balanced Scorecard

	Scorecard Categories	Value Dimension	Measures	Benchmark	Self-Rank 1 - 5	Comments
Business Experience	Innovative	New innovation projects	Profitable value from innovation	Review top performers in market	5	Create and capture sustainable and profitable value from innovation
Personal Experience	Inner Peace	Acceptance of self	Quantity of negative/positive self-talk Time spent meditating	Review meditation master best practices	5	Inner peace means you accept yourself the way you are spirit, soul, and body
1						
2						
3						
4						
5						
6						
7						

Rank Options:
5 – critical to success/key metric
4 – important
3 – somewhat important
2 – useful metric to track
1 – might percolate up in usefulness in the future

Developing a strong and authentic soul signature as a leader requires self-awareness, reflection, and a deep understanding of one's values and strengths. When a leader is aligned with their soul signature, they are more likely to lead with purpose and conviction, inspire their team, and make a positive impact in their organization and beyond.

CHAPTER EIGHT

Building Strong Teams

"Take your needle, my child, and work at your pattern; it will come out a rose by and by. Life is like that—one stitch at a time taken patiently and the pattern will come out all right like the embroidery."
— Oliver Wendell Holmes

In this chapter, we will explore the principles of team building and how they can be applied in an enlightened heart leadership context. We will discuss the importance of diversity and inclusivity in team building and how leaders can encourage collaboration and open communication among team members. As a leader, building strong teams is one of the most critical aspects of your job. Teams that work well together can achieve great things, but building a strong team requires more than just hiring talented individuals. It requires creating an environment that fosters collaboration, trust, and respect.

Illustration: Shutterstock

In this essay, we will explore how leaders can use an enlightened heart approach to build strong teams. In the realm of enlightened heart leadership, the focus extends beyond individual achievements and embraces the power of collaborative efforts. Enlightened heart leaders recognize that high-performance teams are essential for achieving extraordinary results and fostering a culture of growth, innovation, and fulfillment. We will explore how enlightened heart leaders cultivate and nurture high-performance teams, leveraging the principles of compassion, empathy, trust, and purpose to unlock the full potential of their team members.

Creating a Culture of Psychological Safety

Enlightened heart leaders understand that psychological safety is the foundation upon which high-performance teams are built. They create a safe and inclusive environment where team members feel comfortable taking risks, expressing their ideas, and challenging the status quo without fear of judgment or retribution. By fostering a culture of psychological safety, leaders encourage open communication, collaboration, and learning, enabling team members to unleash their creativity and contribute their best.

Nurturing Trust and Collaboration

Trust is a cornerstone of high-performance teams, and enlightened heart leaders prioritize its cultivation. They lead by example, demonstrating trustworthiness, integrity, and authenticity in their interactions. Through effective communication, active listening, and empathy, leaders build strong relationships with team members, fostering a sense of trust and mutual respect. They also create opportunities for team members to collaborate, emphasizing the power of collective intelligence and diverse perspectives in solving problems and driving innovation.

Fostering Growth and Development

Enlightened heart leaders understand the importance of personal and professional growth in building high-performance teams. They invest in the development of their team members, providing mentorship, coaching, and resources to support their growth journeys. Leaders encourage a culture of continuous learning and skill development, recognizing that when team members are empowered to expand their capabilities, they contribute to the overall performance and success of the team.

Cultivating a Shared Purpose

Enlightened heart leaders create a compelling and inspiring shared purpose that aligns with the values and mission of the organization. They communicate this purpose with clarity and enthusiasm, ensuring that team members understand the meaningful impact of their work. By connecting individual roles and responsibilities to the larger purpose, leaders instill a sense of meaning and fulfillment in their team members, fueling their motivation and commitment to achieving exceptional results.

Encouraging Open Communication and Feedback

Effective communication and feedback channels are crucial for building high-performance teams. Enlightened heart leaders create an environment where open communication is encouraged and feedback is seen as an opportunity for growth and improvement. They promote constructive dialogue, active listening, and the exchange of ideas, fostering an atmosphere of trust and collaboration. Leaders also provide timely and specific feedback, recognizing and celebrating team members' achievements, while also providing guidance for growth and development.

Embracing Diversity and Inclusion

Enlightened heart leaders recognize the value of diversity and inclusion in building high-performance teams. They embrace and celebrate individual differences, fostering an environment where everyone feels valued and included. By harnessing the power of diverse perspectives, experiences, and backgrounds, leaders enable teams to approach challenges from multiple angles, driving innovation and creative problem-solving.

Promoting Work-Life Balance and Well-Being

Enlightened heart leaders understand the importance of work-life balance and well-being in sustaining high-performance teams. They prioritize the holistic well-being of team members, promoting practices that support physical, mental, and emotional health. Leaders encourage self-care, stress management, and work-life integration, recognizing that when team members feel supported and balanced, they are more engaged, motivated, and productive. Enlightened heart leaders recognize that high-performance teams are the driving force behind organizational success and transformation. Through a combination of fostering psychological safety, nurturing trust and collaboration, promoting growth and development, cultivating a shared purpose, encouraging open communication and feedback, embracing diversity and inclusion, and promoting work-life balance and well-being, enlightened heart leaders create an environment where teams thrive and unleash their full potential. By embodying the principles of compassion, empathy, and purpose-driven leadership, they build high-performance teams that not only achieve exceptional results but also create a positive and meaningful impact on individuals, organizations, and society as a whole.

Enlightened heart leadership recognizes the significance of diversity and inclusion as fundamental components of a thriving and high-performing organization. It goes beyond merely acknowledging visible differences such as race, gender, age, or ethnicity and extends to embracing a wide range of perspectives, experiences, backgrounds, and abilities. In this essay, we explore how enlightened heart leaders actively support and promote diversity and inclusion, understanding that it not only enhances organizational success but also fosters innovation, creativity, and a sense of belonging among team members.

Embracing and Celebrating Differences

Enlightened heart leaders deeply value and appreciate the unique qualities that diversity brings to a team and an organization. They create an inclusive culture where individuals from all backgrounds feel welcomed, respected, and valued. By embracing and celebrating differences in perspectives, ideas, and experiences, leaders create an environment where every team member can bring their authentic selves to work and contribute their unique strengths to the collective effort.

Building an Inclusive Culture

Enlightened heart leaders are committed to building an inclusive culture where everyone has an equal opportunity to thrive. They establish policies, practices, and structures that promote fairness, equity, and inclusivity. By actively working to eliminate biases and barriers, they ensure that diversity is not just tolerated but actively encouraged and supported. Through their actions and decisions, they foster a sense of belonging, where individuals feel empowered to contribute their best work and ideas.

Promoting Diverse Representation

Enlightened heart leaders understand the importance of diverse representation in all levels of the organization, including leadership positions. They recognize that diverse perspectives in decision-making lead to more innovative solutions and better outcomes. These leaders actively seek out and support diverse talent, implementing inclusive recruitment and promotion practices. By providing opportunities for underrepresented groups to succeed and excel, they create a workforce that reflects the diversity of the broader society.

Providing Education and Awareness

Enlightened heart leaders invest in education and awareness programs to foster understanding and appreciation of diversity. They provide training and resources to enhance cultural competency, unconscious bias awareness, and inclusive leadership skills. By promoting empathy, understanding, and respectful communication, they create an environment where diverse perspectives are valued and conflicts are resolved constructively. These leaders actively encourage continuous learning and self-reflection among team members to deepen their understanding of diversity and inclusion issues.

Encouraging Open Dialogue

Enlightened heart leaders create space for open and honest dialogue about diversity and inclusion. They foster an environment where team members feel comfortable discussing sensitive topics, sharing their experiences, and challenging biases. By encouraging open dialogue, leaders promote learning, growth, and a deeper understanding of different perspectives. They facilitate conversations that lead to increased awareness and empathy, allowing team members to broaden their perspectives and foster a culture of inclusivity.

Empowering Employee Resource Groups

Enlightened heart leaders support and empower employee resource groups (ERGs) that focus on specific dimensions of diversity, such as race, gender, LGBTQ+ inclusion, or disability awareness. They provide resources, platforms, and funding for ERGs to create safe spaces for networking, mentoring, and advocating for the needs and concerns of diverse employees. These leaders recognize the importance of ERGs in fostering a sense of belonging, promoting professional development, and driving positive change within the organization.

Holding Leaders Accountable

Enlightened heart leaders hold themselves and other leaders accountable for fostering diversity and inclusion. They set measurable goals and benchmarks to track progress, create a sense of urgency around diversity initiatives, and ensure that diversity and inclusion efforts are integrated into the organization's strategic objectives. These leaders regularly assess and evaluate their progress, seeking feedback from employees and making necessary adjustments to further support diversity and inclusion.

Leveraging Diversity for Innovation

Enlightened heart leaders understand that diverse perspectives fuel innovation and creativity. They actively seek input from diverse team members and encourage collaboration across different backgrounds and experiences. By creating opportunities for diverse voices to be heard and valued, they tap into the richness that diversity brings to problem-solving and decision-making processes. These leaders foster an environment where all individuals feel empowered to contribute their unique insights, leading to more innovative and effective outcomes.

   Through enlightened heart leadership, organizations can create an environment that embraces and supports diversity and inclusion. By embracing differences, building an inclusive culture, promoting diverse representation, providing education and awareness, encouraging open dialogue, empowering employee resource groups, holding leaders accountable, and leveraging diversity for innovation, enlightened heart leaders foster an inclusive work environment where individuals feel valued, respected, and empowered to contribute their best. This not only drives organizational success but also cultivates a sense of belonging and fulfillment among team members, leading to greater engagement, collaboration, and overall well-being.

Building strong teams begins with embracing diversity and inclusion. When teams are diverse, they bring a variety of perspectives and experiences to the table, which can lead to more innovative solutions and better decision-making. Leaders who approach team building with an enlightened heart understand that diversity and inclusion are not just buzzwords but essential components of creating a strong team. To embrace diversity and inclusion, leaders can:

- Foster a Culture of Respect: Leaders who create a culture of respect where everyone feels valued and heard can create a strong team.
- Encourage Open Communication: Leaders who encourage open and honest communication can foster a culture of trust and collaboration.
- Celebrate Differences: Leaders who celebrate the differences among team members can create an environment where everyone feels comfortable being themselves.

Building a strong team also requires creating a shared vision. When team members have a clear understanding of their team's purpose, values, and goals, they can work together more effectively. To create a shared vision, leaders can:

- Involve Team Members in the Vision-Setting Process: Leaders who involve team members in the vision-setting process can create a sense of ownership and commitment to the team's goals.
- Communicate the Vision Clearly: Leaders who communicate the team's vision clearly and consistently can ensure that everyone is on the same page.
- Align Individual Goals with the Team's Goals: Leaders who align individual goals with the team's goals can ensure that everyone is working towards the same objectives.

Building a strong team also requires fostering a sense of belonging. When team members feel like they belong, they are more likely to be engaged and committed to their work. To foster a sense of belonging, leaders can:

- Create Opportunities for Team Bonding: Leaders who create opportunities for team members to get to know each other outside of work can foster a sense of camaraderie and connection.
- Celebrate Team Accomplishments: Leaders who celebrate team accomplishments can create a sense of pride and achievement among team members.
- Provide Support and Resources: Leaders who provide support and resources to team members can create a sense of safety and trust.

Building strong teams with an enlightened heart approach requires embracing diversity and inclusion, creating a shared vision, and fostering a sense of belonging. When teams are strong, they can achieve great things, but building a strong team requires ongoing effort and attention. By approaching team building with an enlightened heart, leaders can create an environment that fosters collaboration, trust, and respect, leading to more engaged, motivated, and effective teams.

CHAPTER NINE

Leading Change

"Each day has a new canvas to paint upon. Make sure your picture is full of life and happiness, and at the end of the day you don't look at it and wish you had painted something different."
— Ritu Ghatourey

Change is inevitable, and leaders must be able to adapt to new circumstances and challenges. In this chapter, we will explore how leaders can lead change with compassion and mindfulness. We will discuss the importance of staying flexible and open-minded, and how leaders can create a sense of excitement and motivation among their team members during times of change.

Change is an inevitable part of any organization, and leaders must be able to navigate change effectively to ensure their team's success. In this essay, we will explore how leaders can use an enlightened heart approach to lead change successfully.

Illustration: Shutterstock

The Importance of Emotional Intelligence

Leaders who approach change with an enlightened heart understand the importance of emotional intelligence. Emotional intelligence allows leaders to understand their own emotions and those of their team members, which is critical when leading change. To lead change with an enlightened heart, leaders can:

- Practice Self-Awareness: Leaders who practice self-awareness can regulate their emotions effectively and remain calm during times of change.
- Empathize with Team Members: Leaders who empathize with their team members can understand their concerns and address them effectively.
- Communicate Clearly: Leaders who communicate clearly can help their team members understand why the change is necessary and how it will benefit the organization.

Creating a Sense of Urgency

To lead change successfully, leaders must create a sense of urgency among their team members. Creating a sense of urgency helps team members understand why the change is necessary and motivates them to take action. To create a sense of urgency, leaders can:

- Communicate the Need for Change: Leaders who communicate the need for change clearly and consistently can help their team members understand why the change is necessary.
- Provide a Clear Vision for the Future: Leaders who provide a clear vision for the future can help their team members understand what the organization will look like after the change is implemented.
- Set Realistic Goals and Timelines: Leaders who set realistic goals and timelines can help their team members understand what is expected of them and when.

Empowering Team Members

Leading change also requires empowering team members. Empowering team members helps them take ownership of the change and feel invested in its success. To empower team members, leaders can:

- Delegate Responsibilities: Leaders who delegate responsibilities can help team members develop new skills and feel invested in the change.
- Provide Training and Support: Leaders who provide training and support can help team members feel confident in their abilities and prepared to take on new responsibilities.
- Recognize and Reward Progress: Leaders who recognize and reward progress can help team members stay motivated and committed to the change.

Leading change with an enlightened heart approach requires emotional intelligence, creating a sense of urgency, and empowering team members. Change can be challenging, but by approaching it with an enlightened heart, leaders can help their team members navigate it successfully. When team members feel invested in the change and understand its benefits, they are more likely to embrace it and help the organization achieve its goals.

CHANGE WITHIN: LETTING GO

Enlightened heart leadership involves a deep understanding of the importance of letting go and relinquishing control. In this essay, we explore the profound impact of letting go on leadership effectiveness and how it aligns with the principles of enlightened heart leadership. By embracing the concept of letting go, leaders can foster a culture of trust, empowerment, and growth, enabling individuals and organizations to reach their highest potential.

Embracing Impermanence

Enlightened heart leaders recognize that everything is impermanent, including circumstances, relationships, and even their own roles as leaders. They understand that clinging to control and resisting change can hinder growth and innovation. By embracing impermanence, leaders create a mindset that allows them to adapt to evolving situations and make the necessary adjustments to lead effectively. They let go of rigid expectations and instead cultivate a flexible and open-minded approach to leadership.

Letting Go of Ego

Enlightened heart leaders understand the detrimental effects of ego-driven leadership. They recognize that ego can cloud judgment, hinder collaboration, and create a culture of competition and self-interest. By letting go of ego, leaders shift their focus from personal gain to collective success. They empower and support their team members, giving them the autonomy and trust they need to thrive. By setting aside their ego, leaders create an environment where everyone's contributions are valued, fostering collaboration, innovation, and a shared sense of purpose.

Releasing Control

Enlightened heart leaders understand that true leadership is not about controlling every aspect of a situation but about empowering others and fostering their growth. They recognize that micromanagement stifles creativity, diminishes autonomy, and limits the potential of individuals and the organization as a whole. By releasing control, leaders create space for others to step up, take ownership, and contribute their unique skills and perspectives. They provide guidance and support, allowing their team members to explore new ideas, take risks, and learn from both successes and failures.

Letting Go of Past Attachments

Enlightened heart leaders understand the importance of letting go of past attachments and moving forward with a fresh perspective. They recognize that clinging to past successes, failures, or identities can hinder growth and limit new possibilities. By letting go of attachments to the past, leaders create space for innovation and change. They encourage their team members to learn from past experiences, while also embracing new approaches and ideas that can lead to future success.

Cultivating Trust

Letting go is closely tied to cultivating trust within the organization. Enlightened heart leaders understand that trust is the foundation of strong relationships and effective teamwork. They let go of the need to control every decision and instead trust their team members' abilities and judgment. By creating a culture of trust, leaders foster an environment where individuals feel safe to express their ideas, take risks, and learn from their experiences. Trust allows for open communication, collaboration, and the ability to navigate challenges and conflicts with respect and understanding.

Embracing Learning and Growth

Enlightened heart leaders recognize that letting go is a continuous process of learning and growth. They understand that leadership is not about having all the answers but about being open to new perspectives, ideas, and possibilities. By letting go of the need to be the expert, leaders create space for learning from others and embracing diverse viewpoints. They encourage a culture of continuous learning, where individuals are encouraged to expand their knowledge, skills, and abilities.

Letting go is an essential aspect of enlightened heart leadership. By embracing impermanence, letting go of ego, releasing control, relinquishing past attachments, cultivating trust, and embracing learning and growth, leaders create an environment where individuals can thrive, collaborate, and innovate. Letting go allows leaders to create space for new possibilities, empower their team members, and foster a culture of trust, resilience, and adaptability. In doing so, enlightened heart leaders inspire their teams and organizations to reach new heights of success, fulfillment, and collective well-being.

Once a person has the sense of "I need to let this go," that is a sign of their movement into the phase of destruction. Please do not be alarmed. This "letting go" is an essential component to spiritual and emotional growth and is even a sign of growth in a new way of being as a leader. The thought itself is a sign that destruction has begun. It can be around any type of behavior or thought or situation or person. The content of "letting go" is irrelevant. The process is what is being brought about in the person.

The first inclination of the need to let go will be a feeling of dis-ease. You will notice that something that did not bother you before is bothering you now. You might feel a growing irritation where you felt content or calm just a day before. Look for the change in feeling, not the change in context or content. You might notice that an addictive way of thinking or behaving has shown itself in your life. You initially thought that you had the power to curve or stop the behavior but are noticing that you do not. This can be an upsetting awareness. We recommend that you allow the upset to exist and even welcome it into your life. It is merely an indicator of destruction pointing to the next area of growth.

Letting go of the past, releasing the past, or anything else is also about how the mind works. Many who are reading this book likely already know that consciousness is only 6 percent of our brain. This implies that the rest (some 94 percent) represents the unconscious. What that means is that we as humans are inadvertently acting out behaviorally from the unconscious. The fact that we will find ourselves experiencing previous situations and even ourselves in a new and unfamiliar way should not be surprising. This is how it works. We are continually growing in awareness thereby pulling aspects of ourselves out of the unconscious and into awareness.

You literally cannot let go of what you do not yet see. These behaviors reveal themselves in each area of our lives. At work, you might notice that you have an opinion or behave in a way that is different from those around you. Destruction is in noticing that you feel uncomfortable and that you do not want to go along to get along. Many learn from their family of origin that they do, in fact, have to go along to get along so as not to upset the family system. What happens is that many bring that way of being into their adult lives, find themselves in a leadership position, and still believe that having an opinion that differs from those around them is unacceptable. This plays out in companies all around the world and leads to disastrous consequences including corporate misconduct and bankruptcy.

Another way of looking at this is to notice that we are disconnected from the various facets and the various layers that run in us. Even as simple as when somebody asks you, how are you, we robotically answer good, fine, or okay rather than just taking a moment to answer. A person might have health issues, a family member in the hospital, and someone close who just died. They may have final rituals on the weekend and people come over to the house to mourn. With all of this happening a person just answers the question "I'm okay" and goes about their day. This example shows how we can experience destruction as an internal phenomenon. A person will be in a leadership role and have layers of self-experience running internally in the background of external situations. The idea is the same regardless of the context. We can't release what we are not noticing. One reason we don't notice is due to being disconnected from ourselves. Destruction is about breaking down the barriers that keep us disconnected and move us into a more whole and connected way of being.

In the realm of leadership, individuals may feel disconnected from themselves due to societal pressures to conform to certain expectations. They may feel that they need to hide certain aspects of themselves in order to appear more professional or authoritative, leading them to show up in a limited way. This disconnect ultimately impedes their ability to fully embody their role as a leader and limits their potential. To address this issue, individuals can begin by exploring their past experiences and beliefs. By asking questions such as "What is the story?" and "How is the story showing up?" individuals can start to understand the roots of their fears and limitations. For example, a person who experienced abandonment in their childhood may struggle with fear of rejection and people-pleasing tendencies. As they become more aware of these patterns, they can begin to dissolve the story and move into a state of freedom.

This process of releasing or leveraging the past may involve a shift from a victim mindset to a survivor mindset. When individuals are able to see themselves as survivors, they begin to feel empowered and capable of overcoming obstacles. This shift can be incredibly powerful and can lead to spiritual awakenings or epiphanies that fundamentally change the way individuals view themselves and their potential. As leaders, it is important to detach oneself from situations and examine their source. This allows individuals to recognize when old thoughts or patterns are no longer serving them and to integrate new ways of being. By creating a psychologically safe space for individuals to share their truths, leaders can help individuals to overcome their fears and limitations and to embrace all facets of themselves. Ultimately, leadership involves a deep understanding and connection to oneself, as well as a willingness to release or leverage the past in order to move forward. By embracing all facets of themselves and creating safe spaces for others to do the same, individuals can become truly great leaders who inspire others to do the same.

Letting go can be one of the most difficult things to do, especially when it comes to our deeply held beliefs and perspectives. As we go through the process of understanding and embodying a new idea or concept, we may encounter resistance and struggle to truly let go of our old ways of thinking. But as we continue to deepen our understanding and awareness, we may start to see how these beliefs are holding us back and preventing us from experiencing true growth and transformation. It takes courage and vulnerability to confront these beliefs and to let them go, but in doing so, we open ourselves up to new possibilities and perspectives. As we support and guide others on their own journey of letting go, it's important to remember that sound and color must come together. We need to approach this process with both empathy and creativity, using a range of tools and techniques to help others break down their own limiting beliefs and embrace new ideas and perspectives. Through this process, we can help others find the courage to let go and experience true transformation.

PERSEVERANCE

Perseverance is a crucial aspect of leadership that is often overlooked. It requires a deep understanding of one's own motivations and the ability to stay committed to a goal, even when faced with setbacks and obstacles. It is a mindset that enables people to overcome adversity and reach their full potential. Perseverance is a key trait that distinguishes enlightened heart leaders. It is the unwavering commitment, determination, and resilience to overcome challenges and obstacles in pursuit of a greater vision. In this essay, we explore how perseverance intertwines with enlightened heart leadership, highlighting its significance in achieving long-term success, inspiring others, and creating positive change. Through perseverance, leaders demonstrate their dedication to their purpose, empower their teams, and navigate the complexities of leadership with unwavering resolve.

The Power of Resilience

Enlightened heart leaders understand that setbacks and failures are part of the journey. They embrace challenges as opportunities for growth and learning rather than insurmountable barriers. Perseverance allows leaders to bounce back from adversity, adapt to change, and maintain focus on their goals. They inspire their teams to develop resilience by fostering a culture that values continuous improvement, learning from setbacks, and embracing the mindset that obstacles are stepping stones toward success.

Staying Committed to Purpose

Enlightened heart leaders are driven by a deep sense of purpose that goes beyond personal gain. They are unwavering in their commitment to a vision that is rooted in values and serves a greater cause. Perseverance fuels their determination to fulfill that purpose, even in the face of daunting challenges. They inspire and motivate their teams by exemplifying dedication, consistently reminding them of the organization's mission, and instilling a shared sense of purpose that galvanizes collective effort and resilience.

Navigating Uncertainty and Change

In the dynamic and ever-evolving landscape of leadership, enlightened heart leaders understand the importance of perseverance in navigating uncertainty and change. They anticipate and embrace the inevitability of change, and instead of being deterred, they see it as an opportunity for growth and innovation. Perseverance allows leaders to adapt their strategies, seek new perspectives, and make well-informed decisions, even in the face of ambiguity. They inspire confidence in their teams, assuring them that challenges are surmountable and change can be embraced with open minds and hearts.

Inspiring Others

Enlightened heart leaders serve as role models of perseverance, inspiring others through their actions and unwavering dedication. They lead by example, showing their teams that obstacles can be overcome and goals can be achieved through persistent effort. By sharing their own stories of perseverance and vulnerability, leaders create a sense of connection and authenticity that motivates and empowers others to persevere in their own endeavors. They provide support, encouragement, and resources to help individuals overcome obstacles, building a culture of collective perseverance and mutual support.

Embracing Continuous Learning

Perseverance is closely intertwined with continuous learning and growth. Enlightened heart leaders understand that growth comes from embracing challenges, seeking feedback, and being open to new ideas. They encourage their teams to embrace a growth mindset, view setbacks as learning opportunities, and continuously improve their skills and knowledge. By promoting a culture of continuous learning, leaders cultivate resilience, adaptability, and perseverance among their team members, enabling them to navigate complex situations with confidence and tenacity.

Celebrating Milestones and Progress

Enlightened heart leaders recognize the importance of celebrating milestones and progress along the journey. They acknowledge and appreciate the collective efforts and accomplishments of their teams, reinforcing a sense of purpose and motivation. By celebrating small victories, leaders energize their teams, boost morale, and foster a positive and supportive environment. This practice of acknowledging progress serves as a reminder of the value of perseverance and encourages individuals to continue their pursuit of excellence.

Perseverance is an essential characteristic of enlightened heart leadership. It empowers leaders to overcome obstacles, stay committed to their purpose, navigate change, inspire others, embrace continuous learning, and celebrate progress. Through perseverance, leaders not only achieve their goals but also cultivate a culture of resilience, adaptability, and growth within their teams and organizations. By embodying the spirit of perseverance, enlightened heart leaders create an environment that fosters collective perseverance, empowers individuals, and paves the way for long-term success and positive transformation.

Perseverance is about much more than just sticking to a task or project until it is completed. It involves a broader awareness of one's own values and priorities and a willingness to make difficult decisions when necessary. For many people, perseverance means reconciling with relationships or organizations that they may have outgrown. It's about finding a way to move forward while maintaining one's integrity and recognizing the broader meaning of our lives. Successful people understand that perseverance requires mental toughness and discipline. It's about having the courage to take big, bold steps and make changes when necessary. It means setting goals and working towards them, even when the going gets tough. Perseverance requires focus, determination, and a willingness to put in the work required to achieve success.

Unfortunately, many people are held back by old mental mindsets and maladaptive thinking patterns that keep them stuck. These patterns often develop early in life and are reinforced over time, leading people to believe that they are incapable of change. However, with the right mindset and approach, it is possible to break free from these patterns and develop the mental toughness necessary to persevere.

One way to build mental toughness is by developing micro habits. These are small, manageable actions that are so easy to accomplish that they seem almost silly. For example, committing to doing one push-up per day may seem insignificant, but it can help build the momentum needed to achieve larger goals. Micro habits help break down old patterns and reinforce new, more positive ones.

Another challenge to perseverance is our subconscious mind, which often drives our behaviors without us even realizing it. These subconscious patterns can be difficult to recognize and change, but it is possible with the right mindset and approach. By recognizing the root cause of our behaviors and making conscious decisions to modify them, we can shift our focus from external factors to our own internal power.

Ultimately, perseverance is about staying committed to our intentions, even if they don't necessarily result in financial returns. It's about recognizing the broader meaning of our actions and the impact that they have on ourselves and those around us. With an open-minded awareness of our mindset and intentions, we can develop the perseverance necessary to achieve our goals and create a meaningful life. Perseverance is a mindset that enables us to overcome adversity and reach our full potential, both in our personal and professional lives.

KNOWING THE FACTS

In the realm of enlightened heart leadership, the pursuit of truth and knowledge is of paramount importance. Leaders who possess an enlightened heart recognize the significance of knowing the facts and seek to base their decisions and actions on accurate information. In this essay, we explore why it is crucial for leaders to know the facts and how it benefits business outcomes. By embracing the value of truth and knowledge, enlightened heart leaders establish a foundation of credibility, make informed decisions, foster trust among stakeholders, and drive positive business results.

Building Credibility and Trust

Knowing the facts is essential for leaders to establish credibility and earn the trust of their teams, colleagues, and stakeholders. When leaders demonstrate a commitment to seeking and understanding the truth, they build a reputation as reliable and trustworthy individuals. By basing their actions and decisions on solid evidence and accurate information, leaders gain the confidence and respect of those around them. This foundation of credibility and trust allows for open communication, collaboration, and the development of strong relationships, which are vital for achieving business outcomes.

Informed Decision-Making

Enlightened heart leaders understand that knowledge and facts are the bedrock of effective decision-making. By seeking and assimilating relevant information, they are able to make informed choices that consider the complexities and nuances of the situation at hand. Knowing the facts allows leaders to evaluate different options, anticipate potential consequences, and select the most appropriate course of action. Informed decision-making minimizes risks, enhances problem-solving abilities, and increases the likelihood of achieving desired business outcomes.

Transparency and Accountability

Leaders who prioritize knowing the facts foster a culture of transparency and accountability within their organizations. They value honesty and open communication, ensuring that accurate information is shared with stakeholders. By promoting transparency, leaders create an environment where individuals feel comfortable sharing their perspectives and concerns based on factual knowledge. This fosters trust, collaboration, and a shared sense of responsibility for achieving business outcomes. Moreover, leaders who are knowledgeable and accountable for the facts are more equipped to address challenges, resolve conflicts, and hold themselves and their teams accountable for their actions.

Effective Communication

Clear and effective communication is a cornerstone of enlightened heart leadership, and knowing the facts is instrumental in achieving this. Leaders who possess accurate information can articulate their ideas, vision, and expectations with clarity and confidence. They are able to convey complex concepts in a manner that resonates with different audiences and stakeholders. By being well-informed, leaders can engage in meaningful conversations, address concerns, and provide relevant context, fostering understanding, alignment, and effective collaboration among team members. Effective communication facilitates the achievement of business objectives and ensures that everyone is working towards a common goal.

Mitigating Risks and Navigating Challenges

Knowing the facts empowers leaders to identify and mitigate risks effectively. By having a comprehensive understanding of the factors influencing a situation, leaders can anticipate potential challenges and develop proactive strategies to address them. Leaders who are well-informed are better equipped to navigate complex and uncertain environments, making sound judgments and decisions that minimize risks and maximize opportunities. This proactive approach enhances organizational resilience and agility, enabling the business to adapt and thrive in the face of adversity.

Driving Positive Business Outcomes

Ultimately, the knowledge of facts directly contributes to driving positive business outcomes. Informed decision-making, effective communication, transparency, and risk mitigation are all critical factors that impact business performance. Leaders who know the facts can make strategic choices, inspire their teams, and align resources towards achieving organizational goals. By basing their actions on accurate information, enlightened heart leaders can optimize processes, innovate, seize opportunities, and deliver results that benefit the organization, its stakeholders, and its long-term sustainability.

In enlightened heart leadership, knowing the facts is foundational to success. Leaders who prioritize seeking and understanding accurate information gain credibility, make informed decisions, foster trust, drive effective communication, mitigate risks, and ultimately drive positive business outcomes. By embracing a commitment to truth and knowledge, enlightened heart leaders create a culture of integrity, transparency, and accountability, setting the stage for organizational growth, innovation, and long-term success.

The challenge with knowing the facts is that the mind is not designed for that. As you are learning throughout this book, the mind was created to essentially keep us safe. The amygdala, often called the reptile part of the brain, is the oldest part and in charge of scanning the environment to look for threats. Unfortunately, or perhaps fortunately as you might see it, this can create a false sense of knowing. The amygdala is programmed to sort what it sees and download to you, person in body, all perceived threats in any given moment. Now, let's say that you send an email to the executive team regarding a new initiative for the company, and only one out of seven people on the team respond. The amygdala will see that as a threat. The problem is that threats are seen in the mind as something that will cause harm to you as a person. If a person believes this to be a fact, they may react in a way that actually does create harm, such as sending another strongly worded email asking why the lack of response, creating conflict and discord within the executive team. In this example, a lack of a response is not an actual threat. There isn't anything wrong. This seemingly being a threat is not a fact. The mind is not able to distinguish between fact and fiction. Eighty percent of our mental habits are delusional.

People often fall victim to various fallacies of thinking as well. In this example, emotional reasoning will be the likely culprit: "I'm angry, therefore the situation is terrible," or "This person did something wrong." The feeling does not imply fact, and many think that it does. We have old habits wired into our minds, and we must learn the habit of questioning and becoming curious about our thinking. The number one most important habit is to develop curiosity.

FAITH

As leaders, we often get caught up in setting goals, creating action plans, and monitoring key performance indicators. But what if there was a secret formula that successful leaders have been using for years? A combination of self-sovereignty, a passion for making a positive impact on the world, and faith can create a magical concoction that draws the right people and opportunities to form your tribe. Enlightened heart leadership encompasses the harmonious integration of self-sovereignty and faith. Self-sovereignty refers to the empowered sense of self and the ability to make independent choices, while faith pertains to the trust and belief in something greater than oneself. In this essay, we explore how the combination of self-sovereignty and faith relates to enlightened heart leadership, highlighting the importance of personal agency, inner conviction, and a connection to a higher purpose. By cultivating self-sovereignty and embracing faith, leaders can navigate challenges, inspire others, and lead with authenticity and purpose.

Self-Sovereignty—Empowering the Inner Self

Enlightened heart leaders understand the significance of self-sovereignty in their leadership journey. They recognize that cultivating self-awareness, self-empowerment, and personal agency is essential for authentic and impactful leadership. Self-sovereignty enables leaders to tap into their unique strengths, values, and passions, allowing them to lead with authenticity and integrity. By embracing their inner wisdom, enlightened heart leaders are better equipped to make conscious choices, set boundaries, and align their actions with their core values. Through self-sovereignty, leaders gain clarity of purpose, develop resilience, and inspire others to discover their own inner power.

Faith—Trust in Something Greater

Faith, in the context of enlightened heart leadership, goes beyond religious or spiritual beliefs. It encompasses a deep trust and belief in something greater than oneself, whether it be a higher purpose, universal principles, or the interconnectedness of all beings. Faith provides leaders with a sense of grounding and perspective, enabling them to transcend ego-driven motivations and make decisions guided by a larger vision. By cultivating faith, leaders tap into a wellspring of inner strength, resilience, and courage. It allows them to navigate uncertainty, embrace vulnerability, and persevere through challenges, knowing that there is a higher meaning and purpose to their leadership journey.

The Integration—Empowered Leadership with Purpose

The combination of self-sovereignty and faith creates a powerful synergy in enlightened heart leadership. When leaders embrace self-sovereignty, they cultivate the inner strength and conviction necessary to stay true to their values and make decisions aligned with their authentic selves. Simultaneously, faith acts as a guiding force, providing a sense of purpose, inspiration, and trust in the unfolding of events. The integration of self-sovereignty and faith empowers leaders to lead with clarity, compassion, and authenticity.

Authenticity and Personal Alignment

Leaders who embrace self-sovereignty and faith are able to lead with authenticity and personal alignment. They have a deep understanding of their strengths, values, and passions, and they integrate these aspects of themselves into their leadership approach. By staying true to themselves and their beliefs, leaders inspire trust and create a positive and authentic environment where individuals can thrive and contribute their best. The combination of self-sovereignty and faith enables leaders to lead from a place of inner conviction, influencing others through their genuine presence and unwavering commitment to their values.

Resilience and Adaptability

Enlightened heart leaders who embody self-sovereignty and faith are more resilient and adaptable in the face of challenges. They have a strong sense of self and trust in their own abilities, allowing them to navigate uncertainty and overcome obstacles with grace and perseverance. Their faith in something greater than themselves provides them with the resilience to bounce back from setbacks and embrace change as an opportunity for growth. This combination empowers leaders to lead with confidence, navigate complexity, and inspire their teams to embrace challenges with a positive mindset.

Inspiring Others and Building Trust

Leaders who embody self-sovereignty and faith naturally inspire and empower others. By leading with authenticity and personal alignment, they serve as role models, encouraging individuals to embrace their own self-sovereignty and have faith in their abilities. Through their unwavering belief in a greater purpose, they inspire others to connect with something beyond themselves and contribute to a shared vision. The combination of self-sovereignty and faith fosters a sense of trust, as leaders demonstrate their commitment to their values and the well-being of their teams, cultivating an environment of collaboration, open communication, and shared purpose. However, many people overlook the importance of developing a larger vision for themselves and their role on this planet. Understanding your job description on project earth is crucial, and sometimes, letting the universe provide opportunities for success can be the key to unlocking your full potential. Gone are the days of traditional job descriptions and roles. Today, businesses are rapidly shifting their focus to skills. HR professionals should be acquiring talent, not commodities, and retaining top talent is just as important as acquiring it.

Hiring the wrong people is one of the most common problems organizations face. This issue often stems from personal preferences instead of acquiring the necessary skill set for the job. A lack of understanding of human resources from an organizational development perspective can lead to long-standing battles between HR and OD professionals. Today's job market is challenging, with people struggling to read resumes properly and candidates struggling to showcase their unique talents and skills. However, the key to success lies in being in alignment with your divine self and Mother Earth. When all pieces align, a resounding "Y-E-S" signifies that the success algorithm has been activated.

Enlightened heart leadership thrives when self-sovereignty and faith are integrated. By embracing self-sovereignty, leaders cultivate personal agency, authenticity, and alignment with their values. Simultaneously, faith provides a sense of purpose, resilience, and trust in something greater. The combination of these elements empowers leaders to inspire others, navigate challenges with grace, and lead with authenticity and purpose. In the synergy of self-sovereignty and faith, enlightened heart leaders create an environment that fosters growth, collaboration, and positive transformation.

REFLECTION

Developing the habit of reflection is a powerful tool for expanding self-awareness and creating space for new ways of being. As we become more aware, we create the potential for excellence to flourish and expand. This cycle of growth and self-awareness has no end, and it's important to remember that the journey itself is the destination. One key habit to cultivate is a period of reflection each day, particularly upon awakening. This practice creates a structure for the mind, body, and resulting feelings to be held and processed. As we continue to develop our self-awareness, we become more attuned to the gap between our current way of being and where we'd like to be. This awareness unlocks our potential for growth and performance-oriented success. Reflection plays a vital role in enlightened heart leadership, offering leaders the opportunity to deepen self-awareness, gain insights, and make purposeful decisions. In this essay, we explore the significance of reflection in leadership and how it contributes to the development of an enlightened heart. By embracing reflective practices, leaders cultivate a deeper understanding of themselves, their actions, and their impact on others. Through introspection and thoughtful contemplation, leaders can refine their leadership approach, foster personal growth, and create a positive and transformative environment.

Self-Awareness and Authenticity

Reflection serves as a powerful tool for self-awareness, allowing leaders to gain a deeper understanding of their thoughts, emotions, values, and behaviors. By taking time for introspection, leaders can explore their strengths, limitations, and areas for growth. This self-awareness enables leaders to lead with authenticity, aligning their actions with their values and purpose. Through reflection, leaders gain clarity about their intentions, motivations, and the impact they have on their teams and organizations. Self-awareness, developed through reflection, is foundational for enlightened heart leadership, as it fosters genuine connections, trust, and meaningful relationships.

Learning from Experiences

Reflection provides an opportunity for leaders to learn from their experiences, both successes and failures. By taking the time to analyze past actions and outcomes, leaders can identify patterns, strengths, and areas for improvement. Through reflection, leaders extract valuable lessons that inform their decision-making and shape their leadership approach. Examining past experiences helps leaders recognize what worked well and what could be done differently, enabling continuous growth and development. By embracing reflection, leaders create a culture of learning and improvement, encouraging their teams to do the same.

Mindful Decision-Making

In the fast-paced business environment, leaders often face numerous decisions and pressures. Reflection allows leaders to pause, step back, and engage in mindful decision-making. By taking the time to reflect on available information, potential outcomes, and the alignment with their values and goals, leaders can make more thoughtful and intentional decisions. Reflection enables leaders to consider the broader impact of their choices on stakeholders and the organization as a whole. Through mindful decision-making, leaders prioritize long-term sustainable outcomes over short-term gains, embodying the values of enlightened heart leadership.

Empathy and Emotional Intelligence

Reflection cultivates empathy and emotional intelligence—key attributes of enlightened heart leadership. By reflecting on their own emotions and experiences, leaders develop a deeper understanding of their own feelings, which enhances their ability to empathize with others. Through introspection, leaders become more attuned to the needs, perspectives, and emotions of their team members and stakeholders. This heightened empathy enables leaders to create an inclusive and supportive environment where individuals feel seen, heard, and valued. Emotional intelligence, nurtured through reflection, helps leaders navigate conflicts, build strong relationships, and inspire collaboration.

Strategic Thinking and Visionary Leadership

Reflection provides leaders with the space to engage in strategic thinking and visionary leadership. By reflecting on the bigger picture and long-term goals, leaders can evaluate the alignment between their actions and the organizational vision. Reflection enables leaders to assess the progress made, identify areas for improvement, and envision future possibilities. It helps leaders recognize patterns, anticipate challenges, and proactively adapt their strategies. Through reflection, leaders foster a sense of purpose and direction, guiding their teams towards a shared vision and inspiring them to reach their fullest potential.

Personal Growth and Continuous Improvement

Reflection is a catalyst for personal growth and continuous improvement. By engaging in regular reflection, leaders acknowledge their own strengths and areas for development. They are open to feedback, embrace challenges as opportunities for growth, and demonstrate a commitment to self-improvement. Through reflection, leaders cultivate a growth mindset, actively seeking opportunities to learn and evolve. This dedication to personal growth sets an example for their teams, fostering a culture of continuous improvement and excellence.

Reflection is a transformative practice that plays a central role in enlightened heart leadership. By engaging in reflection, leaders deepen their self-awareness, learn from experiences, make mindful decisions, cultivate empathy, and embrace strategic thinking. Through reflection, leaders nurture their own personal growth while creating an environment that encourages learning, innovation, and meaningful connections. By embracing reflective practices, leaders embark on a journey of self-discovery, self-improvement, and enlightened heart leadership, ultimately fostering a positive and transformative impact on individuals, teams, and organizations. To become a leader with a holistic view, it's essential to develop wisdom across all facets of life. This requires discipline and a decision to put oneself in a position to understand each facet of life and reflect on how it contributes to our sense of self. Wisdom is not only gained from experience but also from doing something outside of ourselves, developing foresight and insight into our present and future. However, it's important to recognize that we can't work on something that we aren't aware of. Our generational beliefs may limit our ability to reflect and grow, but developing a daily practice of reflection can help us break free from these limitations and unlock our full potential. By cultivating a sense of self-awareness and wisdom, we can become well-rounded leaders with a holistic view of the world.

PRODUCTIVITY AND SUSTAINMENT

Value is about something important to us and represents what we want. The values that organizations put out describe their mindset. If one has values like open communication in innovation, creation, and creativity, one is in an innovative or growth mindset. However, when one speaks about values like respect and integrity, it results from something that has occurred in the organization. It could be from a leader's observation within the organization which led to identifying those particular values as important or something that needs to be addressed. By adopting an enlightened heart leadership approach, leaders can create a more positive and supportive work environment, foster greater creativity and innovation, and ultimately, achieve greater success for themselves and their organizations.

Enlightened heart leadership is a powerful approach to leadership that emphasizes compassion, mindfulness, and emotional intelligence. It is an approach that recognizes the interconnectedness of all things and seeks to create positive change in the world by leading with heart and wisdom. Throughout this book, we have explored the key principles and practices of enlightened heart leadership, from creating a culture of compassion and self-care to leading change with emotional intelligence and empowering team members. We have seen how leaders can apply these principles and practices to create thriving organizations that benefit everyone involved. Enlightened heart leadership is not just about achieving success in business; it is about creating positive change in the world. It is about recognizing that we are all interconnected and that the actions we take as leaders have a ripple effect that can impact countless others. By leading with an enlightened heart, we can create a world that is more compassionate, just, and sustainable. As we have seen throughout this book, enlightened heart leadership requires ongoing practice and development. It is not something that can be mastered overnight, but rather a lifelong journey of growth and transformation. By embracing this journey and committing ourselves to continual learning and development, we can become more effective and compassionate leaders who create positive change in the world.

An enlightened heart is vital in the future of leadership for several reasons:

- Empathy and Compassion are Key Leadership Skills: In today's complex and rapidly changing world, leaders need to be able to connect with and understand the needs of diverse stakeholders. An enlightened heart enables leaders to empathize with others and approach decision-making with a focus on the well-being of all stakeholders, not just the bottom line.
- Authenticity Builds Trust: Authenticity is a hallmark of enlightened leadership. When leaders are true to themselves and their values, they build trust with their team members, customers, and other stakeholders. This trust is essential for creating a culture of innovation, collaboration, and high performance.
- Mindfulness Supports Resilience and Adaptability: The future of leadership requires leaders to be resilient and adaptable in the face of uncertainty and change. Mindfulness practices such as meditation and self-reflection can help leaders to cultivate the inner resources they need to navigate challenges with grace and flexibility.
- Positive Leadership Promotes Well-Being: Enlightened leaders recognize that their team members are whole human beings with complex needs and desires. By promoting well-being in the workplace through positive leadership practices, they can create a culture where team members thrive, feel valued, and are motivated to contribute their best work.

HEARTFELT LEADERSHIP

An enlightened heart is vital in the future of leadership because it enables leaders to connect with and understand others, build trust, cultivate resilience, and promote well-being. By prioritizing these qualities and practices, leaders can create a more positive, productive, and sustainable future for themselves and their organizations.

CHAPTER TEN

Cultivating Enlightened Heart Leadership for Positive Impact

"You just have to turn the page. It's tough knowing what has happened in the past and how close we've been, but you can't dwell in the past. This is the time to require a new chapter for the future. Hopefully we put ourselves in a position where we will be happy."
— Donovan McNabb

In this final chapter, we will summarize the key concepts discussed throughout the book and highlight the importance of enlightened heart leadership in today's fast-paced and ever-changing work environment. We will encourage readers to reflect on their own leadership style and consider how they can incorporate the principles of mindfulness, compassion, empathy, and emotional intelligence in their own leadership roles. Finally, we will provide some

Illustration: Shutterstock

practical tips and strategies for readers who are interested in adopting an enlightened heart leadership approach in their own organizations.

Enlightened heart leadership is a transformative and holistic approach to leading that emphasizes the integration of key principles and practices. Throughout this book, we have explored the core components of enlightened heart leadership, delving into the profound impact they have on individuals, teams, and organizations. By nurturing self-awareness, fostering empathy, embracing mindfulness, cultivating resilience, committing to continuous learning, and aligning actions with a sense of purpose, enlightened heart leaders can create a positive and lasting impact in their spheres of influence. Self-awareness serves as the foundation of enlightened heart leadership. Through self-reflection and introspection, leaders gain a deeper understanding of their own values, strengths, weaknesses, and biases. This heightened self-awareness enables them to lead with authenticity, align their actions with their core values, and make conscious choices that positively impact their teams and organizations. By continuously exploring their own beliefs and motivations, enlightened heart leaders develop a strong sense of self, which allows them to navigate challenges with integrity and authenticity.

Empathy is a cornerstone of enlightened heart leadership. By cultivating empathy, leaders develop the ability to understand and connect with the experiences, emotions, and perspectives of others. This empathetic understanding fosters an inclusive and supportive environment where individuals feel valued, heard, and empowered. Through active listening, compassion, and a genuine concern for the well-being of their team members, enlightened heart leaders create a culture of trust, collaboration, and shared success.

Mindfulness plays a critical role in enlightened heart leadership. By practicing present-moment awareness, leaders cultivate a deep sense of clarity, focus, and intentionality. Mindful leaders are able to approach situations with a calm and centered mindset, allowing them to make wise decisions, manage conflicts effectively, and inspire others through their presence. By being fully present and attentive, enlightened heart leaders create space for reflection, creativity, and innovation, driving organizational growth and transformation.

Resilience is a fundamental characteristic of enlightened heart leadership. Leaders who embody resilience possess the ability to bounce back from setbacks, adapt to change, and maintain a positive mindset in the face of adversity. By modeling resilience, enlightened heart leaders inspire their teams to embrace challenges, learn from failures, and persevere towards shared goals. This resilience fosters a culture of continuous improvement, growth, and innovation, propelling the organization forward even in the face of obstacles.

Continuous learning is essential for enlightened heart leaders. By recognizing that knowledge and skills are not static, leaders embrace a growth mindset and commit to ongoing personal and professional development. They seek out opportunities to expand their knowledge, challenge their assumptions, and gain new perspectives. By fostering a learning culture within their teams and organizations, enlightened heart leaders encourage others to embrace a mindset of curiosity, exploration, and continuous improvement, leading to enhanced creativity, innovation, and adaptability.

Aligning actions with a sense of purpose is a key aspect of enlightened heart leadership. Leaders who have a clear vision and align their actions with their purpose inspire and motivate their teams to achieve extraordinary results. By communicating their vision with clarity, setting meaningful goals, and aligning individual and team efforts, enlightened heart leaders create a sense of shared purpose and meaning. This sense of purpose ignites passion, commitment, and engagement among team members, fostering a culture of high performance and achievement.

Enlightened heart leadership is a powerful and transformative approach that goes beyond traditional notions of authority and power. By nurturing self-awareness, cultivating empathy, embracing mindfulness, fostering resilience, committing to continuous learning, and aligning actions with a sense of purpose, enlightened heart leaders create a positive and empowering environment where individuals can thrive, teams can flourish, and organizations can achieve sustainable success. By embodying these core components, enlightened heart leaders have the capacity to make a profound and lasting impact, driving positive change in individuals, teams, organizations, and society as a whole.

Overall, this book aims to provide readers with a comprehensive understanding of enlightened heart leadership and how it can be applied in various contexts. Through the exploration of key principles and practical strategies, readers will be equipped with the knowledge and tools necessary to become more effective and compassionate leaders.

WORKBOOK

Cultivating Enlightened Heart Leadership

Welcome to the "Cultivating Enlightened Heart Leadership" workbook. This workbook is designed to help you integrate the principles and practices of enlightened heart leadership into your daily life and leadership approach. It provides actionable steps, reflection exercises, and practical tools to support your journey towards becoming an enlightened heart leader. By engaging with the workbook, you will deepen your self-awareness, cultivate empathy, embrace mindfulness, foster resilience, commit to continuous learning, align actions with purpose, and ultimately create a positive impact as a leader. Let's begin!

Self-Awareness:

- Reflect on Your Values: Identify your core values and consider how they align with your leadership style and decision-making process.
- Assess Your Strengths and Weaknesses: Take inventory of your strengths and weaknesses as a leader and create a plan to leverage your strengths and address areas for improvement.
- Explore Your Beliefs and Biases: Examine your beliefs and biases that may impact your leadership approach and commit to challenging and expanding your perspectives.

Empathy:

- Practice Active Listening: Engage in active listening by fully focusing on the speaker, withholding judgment, and seeking to understand their perspective without interruption.
- Develop Empathy through Perspective-Taking: Put yourself in others' shoes and imagine their experiences, challenges, and emotions. Cultivate a genuine sense of care and concern for their well-being.

Illustration: Shutterstock

- Foster a Culture of Inclusivity: Create an inclusive environment where everyone feels valued, respected, and heard. Encourage diverse perspectives and create opportunities for dialogue and collaboration.

Mindfulness:

- Cultivate Present-Moment Awareness: Practice mindfulness techniques such as meditation, deep breathing, or body scans to bring your attention to the present moment and enhance your focus and clarity.
- Integrate Mindfulness into Daily Activities: Bring mindfulness into your everyday tasks by paying attention to your thoughts, emotions, and actions. Notice any automatic reactions and choose deliberate responses.
- Create Moments of Reflection: Set aside dedicated time for reflection and self-inquiry. Journaling, guided reflection exercises, or contemplative walks can help deepen your self-awareness and insight.

Resilience:

- Embrace a Growth Mindset: Adopt a mindset that views challenges as opportunities for growth and learning. Cultivate a positive attitude towards setbacks and see them as valuable lessons.
- Develop Coping Strategies: Identify healthy coping mechanisms that support your well-being during stressful times. This may include exercise, practicing self-care, seeking support from others, or engaging in creative outlets.
- Foster a Supportive Environment: Encourage open communication, provide resources for personal growth, and celebrate resilience within your team. Build a culture that promotes psychological safety and supports individual and collective resilience.

Continuous Learning:

- Set Learning Goals: Define specific learning goals aligned with your leadership development. Identify areas where you want to expand your knowledge, skills, and capabilities.

- Seek Diverse Perspectives: Engage with individuals from different backgrounds, industries, and disciplines. Actively seek out their insights, experiences, and ideas to broaden your understanding.
- Create a Learning Plan: Develop a personalized learning plan that includes reading books, attending seminars or workshops, participating in online courses, and seeking mentorship or coaching opportunities.

Purpose Alignment:

- Define Your Leadership Purpose: Reflect on your values, passions, and strengths to clarify your leadership purpose. Create a compelling vision that inspires and guides your actions.
- Align Goals with Purpose: Review your current goals and ensure they align with your leadership purpose. Adjust or refine them as needed to create a clear pathway towards fulfilling your purpose.
- Communicate Purpose with Clarity: Share your purpose with your team, articulate its significance, and help them understand how their work contributes to the broader purpose. Inspire and motivate others by connecting their individual goals to the overarching purpose.

Congratulations on completing the "Cultivating Enlightened Heart Leadership" workbook. By engaging in these exercises and implementing the strategies outlined in each chapter, you have taken significant steps towards becoming an enlightened heart leader. Remember that enlightened heart leadership is a continuous journey of growth and development. Keep practicing self-awareness, empathy, mindfulness, resilience, continuous learning, purpose alignment, and the other core components to nurture your leadership potential and create a positive impact in your sphere of influence. Embrace the transformative power of enlightened heart leadership and watch as it positively shapes your leadership journey and the world around you.

WORKSHEET 1

Self-Awareness

Instructions:

1. Reflect on your values and their alignment with your leadership style and decision-making process.

2. Assess your strengths and weaknesses as a leader.

3. Examine your beliefs and biases that may impact your leadership approach.

Worksheet:

1. List three core values that guide your leadership approach:

    Value 1 ....

    Value 2 ....

    Value 3 ....

2. Reflect on how these values align with your leadership style and decision-making process. Write a brief explanation for each value.

3. Identify three strengths you possess as a leader:

    Strength 1 ....

    Strength 2 ....

    Strength 3 ....

4. Acknowledge three areas for improvement or weaknesses as a leader:

    Weakness 1 ....

    Weakness 2 ....

Weakness 3 ....

5. Reflect on any beliefs or biases that may impact your leadership approach. Write down any beliefs or biases that come to mind and consider how they may influence your decision-making and interactions with others.

....
....
....
....
....
....
....
....
....

6. Complete Values (Big Bold Steps) Balanced Scorecard. (See Chapter 7)

WORKSHEET 2
Cultivating Empathy

Instructions:

1. Practice active listening and engage in perspective-taking.

2. Reflect on ways to foster a culture of inclusivity within your team or organization.

Worksheet:

1. Describe one situation where you actively listened to someone and sought to understand their perspective. What did you learn from this experience?

   ....
   ....
   ....
   ....
   ....
   ....

2. Choose a team member or colleague and imagine their experiences, challenges, and emotions. Write a paragraph that describes what you think they may be going through.

   ....
   ....
   ....
   ....
   ....
   ....

3. List three strategies you can implement to foster a culture of inclusivity within your team or organization. Be specific in your actions.

   Strategy 1 ....

   Strategy 2 ....

   Strategy 3 ....

WORKSHEET 3
Cultivating Mindfulness

Instructions:

1. Practice present-moment awareness and integrate mindfulness into your daily activities.

2. Create moments of reflection for deepening self-awareness.

Worksheet:

1. Describe a recent situation where you consciously practiced present-moment awareness. How did this affect your experience and decision-making in that moment?

   ....
   ....
   ....
   ....
   ....

2. Choose one daily activity (e.g., eating, walking, working) and write down three specific actions you can take to bring more mindfulness into that activity.

   ....
   ....
   ....

3. Set aside dedicated time for reflection and self-inquiry. Write down two reflection questions that will help deepen your self-awareness and insight. Use these questions as a starting point for your moments of reflection.

   ....
   ....

WORKSHEET 4
Building Resilience

Instructions:

1. Embrace a growth mindset and develop healthy coping strategies.

2. Consider ways to foster a supportive environment within your team or organization.

Worksheet:

1. Describe a recent challenge or setback you faced and how you approached it with a growth mindset. What lessons did you learn from this experience?

   ....
   ....
   ....

2. List three healthy coping strategies that you can utilize during stressful times to support your well-being:

   Coping strategy 1 ....
   Coping strategy 2 ....
   Coping strategy 3 ....

3. Reflect on ways you can foster a supportive environment within your team or organization. Write down three actions you can take to promote psychological safety and resilience among team members.

   Action 1 ....
   Action 2 ....
   Action 3 ....

HEARTFELT LEADERSHIP

These worksheets are designed to complement the concepts and exercises outlined in the "Cultivating Enlightened Heart Leadership" workbook. Feel free to print multiple copies of each worksheet as needed and use them to deepen your understanding and application of the principles discussed. Remember to take the time to reflect on your responses and consider how you can incorporate these insights into your leadership journey.

CONCLUSION

Using *Heartfelt Leadership* to Maximize Your Potential

As we conclude this book on enlightened heart leadership, we find ourselves at a pivotal moment in history. The world is experiencing unprecedented challenges and rapid transformations, calling for a new paradigm of leadership that transcends conventional boundaries. Enlightened heart leadership emerges as a guiding light, illuminating the path forward with its principles rooted in wisdom, compassion, and interconnectedness.

Throughout our exploration, we have witnessed the transformative power of enlightened heart leadership in action. We have seen leaders who courageously embraced vulnerability, authenticity, and empathy, forging deep connections with their teams and inspiring them to reach new heights. We have observed organizations that cultivated cultures of trust, collaboration, and purpose, fostering environments where individuals could thrive and contribute their unique gifts. We have recognized the profound impact of mindful decision-making, ethical responsibility, and sustainable practices on the well-being of our planet and future generations.

But the journey does not end here. In fact, it is just beginning. As we step into the future, we must carry the torch of enlightened heart leadership, igniting the flames of transformation in every sphere of influence. We must embark on a collective quest to expand consciousness, recognizing that the well-being of individuals, communities, and the planet are intricately interconnected.

The future of enlightened heart leadership lies in embracing collaboration and co-creation, where diverse voices come together in pursuit of common goals. It lies in ethical technological integration, where innovation is guided by moral values and responsible stewardship of resources. It lies in environmental sustainability, as we strive to heal and protect our planet for future generations. And it lies in transformative education, where lifelong learning becomes a vehicle for personal growth and societal progress.

Each and every one of us has the capacity to be an enlightened heart leader. It begins by turning inward, cultivating self-awareness, and nurturing our own hearts. It continues by extending compassion and empathy to others, creating spaces for growth and empowerment. It flourishes when we become catalysts for positive change, influencing our organizations, communities, and society as a whole.

As we embark on this journey, let us remember that enlightened heart leadership is not a utopian ideal, but a practical and necessary response to the challenges of our times. It requires courage, resilience, and a deep commitment to personal growth. It necessitates embracing discomfort and uncertainty, knowing that true transformation often lies on the other side of fear. It demands continuous learning, unlearning, and relearning as we navigate the ever-evolving landscape of leadership.

Together, let us envision a future where enlightened heart leadership is the norm rather than the exception. Let us inspire one another, hold each other accountable, and create supportive ecosystems that nurture the seeds of compassionate leadership. By doing so, we can co-create a world that honors the inherent dignity and interconnectedness of all beings, where love, empathy, and conscious action guide our endeavors.

The time for enlightened heart leadership is now. The world is waiting, hungry for leaders who can light the way toward a more compassionate, just, and sustainable future. Let us rise to the occasion and step into our power as enlightened heart leaders, embracing the extraordinary opportunity we have been given to shape the course of history.

May our hearts be filled with compassion, our minds with wisdom, and our actions with love as we embark on this transformative journey of enlightened heart leadership. Together, let us illuminate the world with our collective brilliance and create a legacy of positive change for generations to come.

As we reach the end of this book, we stand at the precipice of a new era, where the concept of leadership is undergoing a profound transformation. We have explored the depths of enlightened heart leadership, delving into its core principles and witnessing its remarkable impact on individuals, organizations, and society as a whole. But as with any living philosophy, the journey does not end here. In this final chapter, we will explore what lies ahead, envisioning the future of enlightened heart leadership and its potential to shape our world in the years to come.

- Expanding Consciousness: Enlightened heart leadership is rooted in the understanding that true transformation begins within ourselves. As we move forward, the next step is to cultivate expanded consciousness on a global scale. Leaders must encourage practices that foster self-awareness, empathy, and interconnectedness. By embracing diverse perspectives and nurturing a collective sense of purpose, we can create a harmonious and inclusive world that celebrates our shared humanity.

- Collaboration and Co-Creation: In the coming years, enlightened heart leaders will recognize that collaboration is not just desirable but essential for tackling the complex challenges of our time. They will foster a culture of co-creation, breaking down silos and embracing interdisciplinary approaches. Through partnerships and networks, leaders will harness the collective intelligence and creativity of diverse stakeholders, including employees, customers, communities, and even competitors. Together, we will co-create innovative solutions that address societal issues and lead to sustainable progress.

- Ethical Technological Integration: Technology continues to advance at an exponential rate, shaping our lives and transforming industries. Enlightened heart leaders will navigate this digital landscape with a strong moral compass, ensuring that technological innovations align with ethical values. They will seek to bridge the digital divide, using technology as a tool to empower marginalized communities and foster equitable access to opportunities. By fostering ethical technological integration, leaders can leverage the power of innovation to enhance human well-being and protect the planet.

- Environmental Stewardship: The urgency of the climate crisis demands that enlightened heart leaders prioritize environmental stewardship. They will champion sustainability practices within their organizations, embedding ecological awareness into every aspect of decision-making. These leaders will actively engage in regenerative practices, seeking to restore balance and heal the Earth. By embracing the interconnectedness of all life, they will inspire others to join in the collective effort to preserve our planet for future generations.

- Transformative Education: Enlightened heart leaders understand that education is the catalyst for meaningful change. They will redefine educational systems, emphasizing holistic learning that nurtures the mind, body, and spirit. By cultivating curiosity, creativity, critical thinking, and emotional intelligence, these leaders will empower individuals to become conscious contributors to society. They will encourage lifelong learning, embracing the transformative power of education as a means to shape a more compassionate and enlightened world.

ACTION PLAN

Embracing Enlightened Heart Leadership

1. Self-Reflection and Personal Growth:
   - Commit to a regular practice of self-reflection, introspection, and mindfulness.
   - Seek opportunities for personal growth, such as attending workshops, reading books, or engaging in coaching or mentoring relationships.
   - Embrace vulnerability and authenticity, cultivating a deeper understanding of your own strengths, weaknesses, and values.

2. Cultivating Compassionate Connections:
   - Foster a culture of trust, empathy, and collaboration within your immediate sphere of influence, whether it's your team, organization, or community.
   - Actively listen to others, validate their experiences, and practice empathy.
   - Encourage open dialogue and create safe spaces for diverse voices to be heard.

3. Embracing Collaboration and Co-Creation:
   - Seek out partnerships and collaborations across boundaries, including within your organization, with other organizations, and with stakeholders in your community.
   - Foster an environment that values interdisciplinary approaches and encourages diverse perspectives.
   - Engage in co-creation processes to collectively generate innovative solutions to complex challenges.

4. Ethical Technological Integration:
   - Stay informed about emerging technologies and their potential ethical implications.
   - Advocate for responsible and ethical use of technology within your organization and in society at large.
   - Support initiatives that bridge the digital divide and promote equitable access to technological advancements.

5. Environmental Stewardship:
   - Integrate sustainability practices into your personal and professional life.
   - Assess and reduce the environmental footprint of your organization, promoting eco-friendly practices and initiatives.
   - Advocate for policies and actions that address climate change, protect natural resources, and promote a sustainable future.

6. Transformative Education:
   - Embrace a lifelong learning mindset, seeking opportunities to expand your knowledge and skills.
   - Support educational initiatives that promote holistic learning, emotional intelligence, and critical thinking.
   - Mentor and inspire others to pursue personal and professional growth through education.

7. Leading by Example:
   - Model enlightened heart leadership in your everyday actions and decision-making.
   - Communicate your values and vision, inspiring others to embrace compassionate and conscious leadership.

- Share success stories and lessons learned to inspire and empower others on their own leadership journeys.

8. Building Supportive Networks:
    - Connect with like-minded individuals and communities who are also committed to enlightened heart leadership.
    - Join or create networks, forums, or communities of practice where you can learn from and collaborate with others.
    - Engage in conversations, share insights, and collectively work towards advancing the principles of enlightened heart leadership.

9. Measuring Impact and Iterating:
    - Establish metrics and indicators to assess the impact of your enlightened heart leadership practices.
    - Regularly evaluate and reflect on your progress, identifying areas for improvement and celebrating successes.
    - Continuously iterate and adapt your approach based on feedback and evolving circumstances.

10. Advocacy and Ripple Effects:
    - Use your voice and influence to advocate for enlightened heart leadership principles in your broader community and society.
    - Share your experiences, insights, and knowledge through speaking engagements, writing, or social media platforms.
    - Recognize the ripple effects of your leadership, inspiring others to embrace and embody enlightened heart leadership principles.

Remember, this action plan is just a starting point. Feel free to adapt and customize it to your specific context and aspirations. By taking intentional steps and collectively working towards enlightened heart leadership, we can create a more compassionate, equitable, and sustainable world for all.

In conclusion, enlightened heart leadership is not a destination but an ongoing journey of growth and evolution. It is an invitation for leaders to step into their authentic selves and lead with compassion, wisdom, and purpose. As we move forward, let us embrace the potential that lies within us and commit ourselves to the pursuit of enlightened heart leadership. Together, we can co-create a future where love, empathy, and conscious action guide our endeavors, creating a world that honors the interconnectedness of all beings and fosters the flourishing of the human spirit. The time for enlightened heart leadership is now, and the future is ours to shape.

ABOUT THE AUTHOR

Dr. Laura Williamson

Dr. Laura Williamson is truly passionate about supporting people at any stage and ability to transform their lives. As a researcher, writer, therapist, and faculty member with over twenty articles, book chapters, books, instructional CDs, and professional presentations in publication, she views the process of learning and psychological development through a trauma-informed, family-system, and cognitive-behavioral therapy lens, each of which have been influenced by her extensive training and experience. Several notable influences include Lifespan Integration, "The Work" by Byron Katie, Cognitive Load Theory, Schema Acquisition Theory, and Relational Life Therapy.

Laura is also dedicated to organizational transformation. Recognizing the need for today's organizations to fully integrate knowledge about heart work and trauma into their policies, procedures, and practices, she is passionate about creating business solutions as they present at the intersection of data- and relational-centered systems.

This is no small task, and Laura loves the challenge! Two examples of finding these solutions follow. In an effort to create accessibility for those who would not otherwise pursue a higher education, she created a roadmap for learning and outreach, developing stackable and portable business microcredits around specific study areas, such as finance, HR, accounting, and more. These areas now align with professional certifications—CPA, CMA, CFA, PCM, CAPM, PMP, SHRM-CP, SHRM-SCP, CAP—which are globally recognized and portable and able to reach a diverse student market. For the second example, she established and implemented success metrics for stakeholders internal to the organization and worked with the system to deploy them at scale, revising on a continual basis based on feedback and data. She insisted on the highest standards through creating metrics around instructional, curriculum, and delivery performance, which are now being rolled out to the entire university, resulting in improvement in faculty performance in exceeding standards from 13 percent to 83 percent.

Additionally, Laura holds five degrees: a BA in philosophy, MBA in leadership, EdD in instructional technology, MEd in adult education for diverse learners, and MA in counseling. Her therapeutic work has been with the Eastside Center for Family, YWCA Angeline's Day Center, WA State Women's Correctional Facility, PEER Seattle, and the CityU of Seattle Counseling Center, where she engaged in individual, couples, and group work focusing on addiction, grief and loss, stress management, assertive communication, cognitive distortions, and relapse prevention. Her industry experience includes private sector work with several West Coast firms, including Data I/O Corporation, Boeing Computer Services, Physio-Control, and L-3 Corporation, where she was responsible for a variety of educational technology, technical training, and process improvement projects including the development and delivery of technical manuals, trainings, and programs, using multimedia methodologies such as interactive CD-ROMs, job-aids, reports, and quick reference guides with clients such as the LAPD, the US Coast Guard, and KTLA News in Los Angeles, California, to name a few.

Finally, Laura has worked for over twenty-five years in higher education in the capacity of adjunct faculty, dissertation chair, dissertation committee member, professor, program director, and associate dean. For five universities she has designed and taught courses and programs for online delivery, international, hybrid, ESL, and face-to-face formats using WebCT, eCollege, and Blackboard platforms.

linkedin.com/in/drlaurawilliamson/
drlaurawilliamson.com

ABOUT THE AUTHOR

Dr. Jivi Saran

A pioneer in the field of business strategy consulting and leadership development, Dr. Jivi Saran is a senior business advisor with BDC Financial. She specializes in large-scale change management as well as leadership growth and development. In her role as a professor of leadership studies and organizational behaviour, Dr. Jivi Saran combines leadership expertise with an acute understanding of the dynamics, philosophy, and individual psychology that drive an organization. It's a transformational approach that's being leveraged to turn a new generation of MBA students into self-aware and inspiring leaders of tomorrow.

Dr. Jivi Saran has come to realize the gap in the world of business today is the connection between the business strategy and a leader's personal legacy of how they want to impact the world. She is currently doing a doctorate in business and holds a PhD in spirituality and an MBA specializing in leadership studies. She is a published author of many international best-selling books on leadership including *Permission to Be You* and *Corporate Soul* and co-authored *Peak Performance*.

She is an accomplished keynote speaker on the topics ranging from discovering who you are, the corporate soul, and corporate mindfulness. She has produced and hosted a TV show called "Winds of Change with Jivi" about corporate spirituality. With her 35-year business career and extensive education and experience as a senior business advisor across many industries, she has dedicated her professional life to the human aspect of business strategy.

Dr. Jivi Saran has learned high team performance starts with the peak performance of a leader, so she uses insightful business strategy, her highly developed observational skills, and mental perception of thought processes for discerning the truth about an organizational team to gain powerful creativity, focus, and productivity. She has an extraordinary mind for improving conditions across an organization and has developed some of the most sophisticated and powerful models of leadership, organizational strategy, and mindset improvement through her "Corporate Soul" program. Coined as the "CEO Whisperer," she works closely with high level CEOs to accelerate growth and profitability in their business. Dr. Jivi Saran and her unique set of skills and offerings is changing the game for organizations around the world and is revolutionizing the way organizations view and create business strategy.

linkedin.com/in/jivisaran/

www.ingramcontent.com/pod-product-compliance
Lightning Source LLC
Chambersburg PA
CBHW042024100526
44587CB00029B/4286